POLICE
IN AMERICA

REPORTS
of the
SPECIAL COMMITTEE
APPOINTED TO INVESTIGATE
THE OFFICIAL CONDUCT
of the
MEMBERS of the BOARD
OF POLICE COMMISSIONERS

The Joint Special Committee

ARNO PRESS & THE NEW YORK TIMES
NEW YORK, 1971

Reprint Edition 1971 by Arno Press Inc.

LC# 78-156279
ISBN 0-405-03372-9

Police In America
ISBN for complete set: 0-405-03360-5
See last pages of this volume for titles.

Manufactured in the United States of America

CITY OF BOSTON.

REPORTS

OF THE

SPECIAL COMMITTEE

APPOINTED TO INVESTIGATE THE OFFICIAL CONDUCT OF
THE MEMBERS OF THE BOARD OF

POLICE COMMISSIONERS.

1881.

In COMMON COUNCIL, December 22, 1881.

GENERAL MANAGEMENT OF THE DEPARTMENT.

The Joint Special Committee appointed to investigate the charges contained in an order for the removal of Henry Walker from the office of Police Commissioner, and to whom was referred the petition of said Walker for an investigation of his official acts, beg leave to submit the following

REPORT.

That Mr. Walker substantially claims to have done his duty as a Police Commissioner, by issuing a standing order to the captains, "to see that the laws are enforced;" and the fact that no complaints are made to the Police Commissioners that the laws are not being enforced satisfies him that the department is properly carrying on its work. Mr. Walker says that no special orders are given except upon special cases where complaints are made. Your committee find there are three classes of crime which exist in this city to a very great extent, to wit, the illegal sale of liquor, keeping of houses of ill-fame, and the keeping of gambling-houses; all of which are carried on in such an open manner that the places where such practices exist are known to the police and to the public.

The first-named is carried on throughout the whole city, the last two are confined mainly to the city proper.

Mr. Walker says that during the time he has been a member of the Board there has not been any special order given in regard to either of said classes of crime, except in some particular cases; that the two last classes mentioned, he thinks, should be regulated and kept within certain districts, so as not to spread them out over the entire city, because such evils always will exist, and the only remedy is to regulate them and keep them as quiet and orderly as possible. Mr. Walker says that, whenever he is *officially* notified or complained to concerning any particular place, he issues o 'ders to have the matter examined into. Mr. Walker also says that it is almost an impossibility to prove that a person is guilty of illegally selling liquor.

It was in evidence before your committee that there are houses of ill-fame and gambling-houses in this city that have openly done and are now carrying on the same business and in the same place as for the last eight or ten years without hindrance or molestation from the police.

It was also in evidence that one of the worst localities in the city is now under process of improvement; that within the last few months one of our citizens has moved into and taken up his residence right in the centre of that locality, solely for the purpose of breaking up the bad places there and improving the character of the place; that some of the places have been broken up, and those that remain are preserving something akin to order; that that citizen had tried, by and through the Police Department, to have that locality improved in its morals and relieved of its vicious people, but without success, and had finally come to the conclusion that the only way in which the street could be improved was for him to take hold of the matter personally, move into the place, and then watch the places there, and thus become sufficiently acquainted with the character of the places so as to testify against them in court. The same citizen also testified before your committee that he spoke with each member of the Board of Police Commissioners in regard to that locality; that from Mr. Walker he received no real assistance in the matter, but that Messrs. Jones and Gargan, when he spoke to them on the subject, quickly offered and promptly gave him all the assistance in their power.

There was testimony before your committee that Mr. Walker, in his treatment of citizens who went to him in his official capacity, was discourteous, and that he treated them in such a manner that they left him feeling hurt and as though they had been abused, not on account of their request being refused, but on account of the manner of Mr. Walker towards them.

Mr. Walker was asked specific questions by your committee in regard to various places by which he is daily passing, concerning the business carried on there; but he (Walker) said he could not say anything in regard to it; but your committee knew what the common report was upon the street, and also had testimony from witnesses before the committee, which confirmed the street report; and it was also said to your committee that no person with ordinary intelligence could pass through that locality, during the last three or four years, without seeing that the street report concerning the same was correct.

Your committee learned that there was a feeling in the community against the members of the Police Commission, and that the public believed there was an unjust and improper discrimination made in the granting of liquor licenses; your committee, therefore, examined into the subject, and find that there is an unjust and improper discrimination in the granting of licenses; that all applicants for licenses do not stand on the same footing or have an equal chance of success with others; that, where objection is made by proper and reputable citizens to the granting of any particular license, it is not of any weight if the petitioner can bring a certain amount of influence to bear upon the Board of Police Commissioners. Your committee also find that the construction placed upon the law by Mr. Walker, in regard to the granting of licenses, is to the advantage of the few who have a number of friends that will intercede for them and not for the public. Annexed hereto is a copy of the testimony taken at one of the meetings of the committee upon the subject.

Your committee examined into the question of the sale of liquor, and find that it is openly done in all parts of the city between the hours of midnight and six o'clock A.M., also on the Sabbath, and apparently no determined attempt is made to stop it, or to enforce the law against those who are carrying on such practices.

One of the members of the City Government made a complaint to Mr. Walker against certain members of the Police Department for improper and riotous conduct, and more than three months elapsed before any attempt was made by Mr. Walker to examine into the matter. Mr. Walker said that he forgot it, and that was the reason it had not been attended to before; but Mr. Walker's attention was called to the matter several times during the three months before-mentioned.

Your committee find that Mr. Walker has not attempted to have the laws enforced; that he does not attempt to learn whether they are enforced or not; that, when complaints are made to him of the breaking of the laws, he does not endeavor to stop it; that he does not try to have the members of the department carry out the rules as laid down by the Board; and your committee further find that Mr. Walker has not shown in this investigation that knowledge of the needs and duties of the Police Department that is required of a person who is at its head.

Your committee therefore recommend his removal.

Your committee would also recommend that the Mayor be requested to petition the Legislature for a change in the law whereby the power to grant licenses for the sale of intoxicating liquors shall be vested in some persons who shall not at the same time be members of the Board of Police Commissioners.

> CLINTON VILES,
> CHAS. H. HERSEY,
> JESSE M. GOVE,
> THOMAS N. HART.

THE CASE OF COMMISSIONER WALKER.

The Joint Special Committee appointed to investigate the charges contained in an order for the removal of Henry Walker from the office of Police Commissioner beg leave to submit the following

REPORT.

That it appeared from the evidence introduced before your committee that Mr. Walker appeared before the Municipal Court of the City of Boston for the transaction of criminal business, apparently as counsel for the defendant in a bastardy process; but, from Mr. Walker's testimony, your committee find that he acted in such capacity because he had been informed that a crime of a very grave nature had been committed, and he considered that mode the best way to get at the facts, so as to bring the parties, if guilty of the crime, before the courts, where they could be dealt with according to law.

It also appeared before your committee that Mr. Walker had appeared of record in various courts, as counsel in suits pending in said courts ; but your committee find that in most of said cases where Mr. Walker appears he appears for members of the Police Department who have been sued for acts done as police officers. Mr. Walker says at no time has he tried a case of that kind, nor has he received any compensation for such services so rendered ; that he did it solely for the purpose of saving the officer from expense.

Mr. Walker also says that the other cases which he has tried in court were cases in which he had been employed prior to his appointment as a Police Commissioner, and which his clients preferred he should finish rather than to have other counsel come into the case ; and as there were but few of such cases he had attended to them.

It also appeared in evidence that prior to Mr. Walker's appointment he brought a suit in one of our courts in favor of James Dorr ; that said case was tried by H. E. Swasey, Esq., on Nov. 2d and 3d, 1881, in the Superior Court for this county ; that a letter and telegram were sent by Mr. Walker to said Dorr on the day of their date, copies of which, with a copy of a certificate of the Clerk of the Superior Criminal Court, are hereto annexed : that said Dorr had been arrested and defaulted his bail upon one complaint for the illegal sale of liquor, and that the same had not been settled or disposed of at the time of the trial of said civil action, and that there was another warrant out against said Dorr upon another complaint for the same offence. Mr. Walker, upon inquiry, says, that before the civil case came up he went to the District Attorney and stated the facts in the civil and criminal cases, at the request of Mr. Swasey, and told him that although Dorr had been convicted of " larceny from the person," and had served a sentence for the same, Mr. Walker thought Dorr was innocent of the crime ; and Mr. Walker said he left the whole matter in the hands of the District Attorney as to whether Dorr should be troubled with arrest upon the criminal matter if he came here to attend the trial of the civil case, and the District Attorney did give him permission to come, but did not and could not interfere between Dorr and his bondsmen. Mr. Walker said that he did not think there was anything inconsistent in his acts in that matter, and the duties of his position at the head of the Police Department of the City of Boston.

It also appeared that Wm. Hackett, a member of the police force, and belonging to the liquor squad connected with the department, went to New York in October, 1881, in behalf of Dorr's bondsmen, and also in behalf of the city, to arrest Dorr and bring him back to Boston; but officer Hackett said he could not find Dorr.

It should be said here that your committee do not find that Mr. Walker had any knowledge whatever that Officer Hackett was going to New York.

Your committee therefore find that the charges made have been proven, but that Mr. Walker should be commended for his acts in regard to the case in the Municipal Criminal Court, and also in regard to his acts in cases where police officers had been sued. In regard to Mr. Walker's acts concerning the case of James Dorr your committee find that the same is entirely inconsistent with the duties of his office; that Mr. Walker knew where the fugitive was and suppressed the information, at the same time assisting him to carry on his private business; that, from the testimony before your committee, your committee believe that Mr. Walker has been acting as counsel for said Dorr and knew of his whereabouts, and also knew of these complaints against him ever since the first of these complaints was issued against Dorr by the court. Rule Number 143, in the Manual of the Department, is as follows: "No member shall communicate to any person any information which may enable persons to escape from arrest or punishment, or that may enable them to dispose of or secrete any goods, or other valuable things, stolen and otherwise unlawfully obtained." Mr. Walker says that the Board of Police Commissioners have issued a standing order to the captains of the various stations "to see that the laws are enforced." Your committee therefore find that Mr. Walker has not only acted in a manner inconsistent with his office as a member of the Board of Police Commissioners, but has also violated, both in spirit and letter, his own Rules and Orders; and in the case of James Dorr, instead of assisting in having the laws enforced, Mr. Walker has been instrumental in aiding the fugitive to escape the penalty of his own illegal acts.

Your committee therefore recommend the passage of the order.

CLINTON VILES,
CHAS. H. HERSEY,
JESSE M. GOVE,
THOMAS N. HART.

THE CASE OF COMMISSIONER GARGAN.

The Joint Special Committee appointed to investigate the charges contained in an order for the removal of Thomas J. Gargan from the office of Police Commissioner beg leave to submit the following

REPORT.

That Mr. Gargan appeared before them and made the following statement : That, by reason of overwork, he suffered during the winter months from extreme nervous prostration, and to such a degree that his physician ordered him to leave work and the city, if he wished to live ; that he consulted his physician as to the place where he should go to recuperate his health, and that the Hot Springs of Arkansas was settled upon as being a proper place ; that shortly after that time, but before he left Boston, a proposition was made to him to go to Mexico in behalf of a railroad company, the company agreeing to pay his expenses. He then consulted his physician, and was advised by him that the climate in Mexico would be as beneficial to him as in Arkansas ; and thereupon he obtained permission of the Mayor to go, as he supposed the Mayor was his superior officer, and the proper person to apply to ; and on the 25th day of March, 1881, he left Boston for Mexico, and did not return to Boston until the 26th day of June, 1881. Mr. Gargan further says that during the major part of the time that he was away he was very sick, and that he had but barely recovered when his wife was taken down with a fever, and remained sick until their return ; that he did not receive any compensation from said railroad company excepting the payment of his expenses.

Your committee asked the opinion of the City Solicitor, Mr. Healy, upon the following question : "Has a Police Commissioner the right under the ordinance to absent himself from the city for a period of thirty days without the consent of the City Council having been first obtained?"

To which question Mr. Healy gave the following opinion : "A Police Commissioner has not the right to absent himself from the city and his duties without the consent of the City Council."

Your committee are, therefore, of the opinion that the charge made has been proven ; that although Mr. Gargan says he supposed that the Mayor was his superior officer, to whom he should apply for leave of absence, yet, in the opinion of your committee, that should not have any weight, as, under the statutes of this Commonwealth, the Mayor has the right, only in case of an emergency, to assume command of the whole or any part of the Police Department, thereby showing it was not the intention of the Legislature to leave the matter in doubt as to the superior officer in that department; that the Mayor is not the superior officer, but is granted by statute, in cases of emergency, certain powers, but cannot be construed as the head officer of that department. Furthermore, it takes the concurrent action of both branches of the City Government to confirm the Mayor's appointment for that office, and it seems to your committee that a person who would give any other construction to the statutes and ordinances than the one given by the City Solicitor would be incompetent to perform the duties attendant upon the office of a Police Commissioner of the City of Boston. The Police Commissioners themselves give the same construction; for on page 18, in the Manual issued by order of the Police Commissioners, the following preface appears: "The Police Department of the City of Boston consists of a 'Board of Police Commissioners,' three in number, nominated by the Mayor and confirmed by the City Council, and a 'Police Force' appointed by said Board."

In the opinion of your committee Mr. Gargan has acted in violation of the statutes and ordinances, and should be held strictly accountable therefor; for, when the head of a department will do that which if done by a subordinate would cost the subordinate his position, it is much more necessary that the superior officer should be dealt with, at least, equal severity; for, if the superior officer breaks the law with impunity, and does not suffer by it, he is looked upon with contempt when he attempts to enforce the same rule or law upon others who are his inferior in office, and under our form of government one man, although the highest in office, is as amenable to the law as the poorest and lowest man in the street; but the punishment that should be meted out for breaking the law should fall the heaviest and be most severe upon him, who, by his position, influence, and education, is bound and presumed to know the law.

Therefore your committee recommend the passage of the order.

> CLINTON VILES,
> CHAS. H. HERSEY,
> JESSE M. GOVE,
> THOMAS N. HART.

THE CASE OF COMMISSIONER JONES.

The Joint Special Committee appointed to investigate the charges contained in an order for the removal of Edward J. Jones from the office of Police Commissioner beg leave to submit the following

REPORT.

Your committee, at one of its meetings, voted to request Mr. Jones to furnish the committee with a detailed statement of the number of cases in which he had acted as Bail Commissioner and Commissioner of Insolvency during the period in which he had been a member of the Board of Police Commissioners, together with the amount of fees he had received for such service ; which request Mr. Jones cheerfully complied with.

It appears, by said statement, that Mr. Jones has acted as Bail Commissioner and Commissioner of Insolvency, from April 1, 1880, to June 15, 1881, in seven hundred and thirty-three cases, ninety-eight of which were charity cases, and for which he received no fees ; that, in the other six hundred and thirty-five cases, he received an average fee of $2.00 per case, making a total receipt from the two offices of Bail Commissioner and Commissioner of Insolvency for fourteen and one-half months of $1,270. Mr. Jones says that his office expenses for that period amounted to $600, and Mr. Jones claims that $500 of that sum should be deducted from the $1,270.

Mr. Jones also says that the fees earned by him as Commissioner of Insolvency have been earned between the hours of three o'clock and six o'clock P.M. ; and that the fees earned by him as Bail Commissioner have been earned between the hours of nine o'clock P.M., and four o'clock A.M., and at no time has the taking of bail or acting as Commissioner of Insolvency in any manner interfered with his duties as a Police Commissioner, but rather to the contrary ; for, when he is called to take bail at any of the stations, he has an opportunity of seeing whether or not the officers are attending to their duties, and instructing them in such matters as circumstances may require. Mr. Jones further says that being a Police Commissioner was an assistance to him as Bail Commissioner, because people, knowing him to be one of the Police Commissioners, would be likely to furnish better bail than they otherwise would.

Mr. Jones, in answer to the inquiry as to " whether or not

officers had sent for him to act as Bail Commissioner on account of his being a Police Commissioner," answered "that he had no doubt they had."

Your committee asked the opinion of the City Solicitor, Mr. Healy, upon the following question: "Has a Police Commissioner the right, under the ordinance, etc., to act as Bail Commissioner, or Commissioner of Insolvency, or engage in business of any kind not connected with his office of Police Commissioner, either during office hours or at any other time, for compensation?"

To which question Mr. Healy made the following reply: "The ordinance passed June 14, 1878, provides that the members of the Board of Police Commissioners shall devote their time to the duties of the office, and shall not actively engage in any other business."

Your committee are of the opinion that the charges made have been proven, and that Mr. Jones has been actively engaged in taking bail and acting as a Commissioner of Insolvency, in violation of the ordinance, during the whole time in which he has been a member of the Board of Police Commissioners.

Your committee also find that the offices of Police Commissioner and Bail Commissioner are incompatible, because officers will, as Mr. Jones says he has no doubt they have, send for him to act as Bail Commissioner on account of his being one of the Police Commissioners, and in that way, having rendered a service to the head of their department, there would be a liability of want of proper discipline among those who should get large numbers of bailable cases for the head of the department to officiate in; for the officers would presume that, when they had furnished their superior officer with opportunities to make money, and he had accepted them, they would be dealt with more leniently than others; thus creating jealousy among the officers, so that each would be striving to make as many arrests as possible, in order that his superior officer might get a fee, and the subordinate rise in the estimation and good graces of his superior, thereby opening the door to a great amount of fraud and corruption, and making the rules of the department, which are created for the best interests of the whole city, of no avail; and thus the office of Police Commissioner, which should be above suspicion, would be brought into contempt, and its members have the reputation of being in the market to the highest bidder.

That, although it is claimed by Mr. Jones that a benefit is derived by his going to the various stations to bail people, thereby giving him an opportunity to see that the city's business is being properly carried on, it is not, in the judgment of your committee, of any weight, as it is the duty of the members of the Police Commission to see that the department is properly carrying out the work belonging to it at all times.

It is also claimed by Mr. Jones that better bail is likely to be offered to him as Bail Commissioner, because he is a member of the Police Commission. That may be true ; but, even if true, it is based upon a wrong principle, as it is manifestly improper and wrong for one person at the head of a department, whose duty it is to prosecute those who break the laws of this Commonwealth and the ordinances of the city, at the same time to receive money for services rendered the very party, and upon the same matter which he and his subordinates are prosecuting the party upon.

Mr. Jones says that when he was appointed, in 1880, one of the Police Commissioners, it was for a short term, and he intended, that if he should be appointed for the long term, in 1881, to stop acting as Bail Commissioner ; but your committee find that, although that might have been Mr. Jones' intention in 1880, he has not carried his intention into effect ; for he was appointed one of the Police Commissioners, March 7, 1881, and confirmed March 18, 1881, since which time he has been continually acting as Bail Commissioner.

Mr. Jones also says that if it is the opinion of the City Solicitor that he (Jones) cannot, under the ordinance, legally and properly act as Bail Commissioner and Commissioner of Insolvency, then he will decline any further service in such capacity ; but your committee find that Mr. Jones, when he was appointed to the office, in 1880, had already duly considered the ordinance, and had formed the same opinion that the City Solicitor has, and the only one that your committee think could be given to the ordinance, to wit, "That he could not properly act as Bail Commissioner and Commissioner of Insolvency and Police Commissioner at the same time."

Rule 148 of the rules governing the Police Department prescribes that "each member of the police force shall devote his whole time and attention to the business of the department, and he is expressly prohibited from following any other calling, or being employed in any other business. Although certain hours are allotted to the respective members for the performance of duty on ordinary occasions, yet at all times, when notified, he must be prepared to act immediately." Your committee therefore find that Mr. Jones has knowingly acted in violation of the ordinance of the city, and in violation of the rules established by the Board of

Police Commissioners for the government of that department. Your committee therefore recommend the passage of the order.

CLINTON VILES,
CHAS. H. HERSEY,
JESSE M. GOVE,
THOMAS N. HART.

BOSTON, October 27, 1881.

DEAR SIR: — Your case (Dorr *vs.* Reed) will be on for trial on Monday next, without fail. It cannot be continued again. The District Attorney will not molest you while here for the trial. Can you trust your bail? I'll write again to-morrow (Friday). Answer on receipt, and keep where you can get letters and telegrams from me without delay.   Yours, etc.,

HENRY WALKER.

If you come on you must bring some money for witnesses and for Swasey.

[COPY OF TELEGRAM.]

BOSTON, October 31.

JAMES DORR or THOMAS DORR, *143 M. Lane, N.Y.* — Case on to-morrow. — Come on. — All right. — Don't fail coming.

WALKER.

SUPERIOR COURT,
FOR THE TRANSACTION OF CRIMINAL BUSINESS,
CLERK'S OFFICE, BOSTON, January 9, 1882.

I hereby certify that at the May Term of said Court, A.D. 1880, James Dorr was indicted, tried, and convicted of the crime of larceny from the person, and was sentenced therefor to the House of Correction, in Suffolk County, for the term of one year.

JOHN P. MANNING, *Clerk.*

IN COMMON COUNCIL, December 29, 1881.

Ordered, To be printed, together with the Minority Report, and referred to the next City Council.

Sent up for concurrence.

IN BOARD OF ALDERMEN, December 31, 1881.

Concurred.

Attest:

S. F. McCLEARY,
City Clerk.

MINORITY REPORT.

The undersigned of the Joint Special Committee, to whom was referred, first, the order introduced into the Common Council by Mr. Jesse M. Gove, viz. : —

Whereas Section 2 of the ordinance entitled "An ordinance to establish the salaries of the members of the Board of Police Commissioners of the City of Boston," passed June 14, 1878, prescribes that said Board of Commissioners shall devote their time to the duties of the office, and shall not actively engage in any other business ; and

Whereas Edward J. Jones, one of the members of said Board of Police Commissioners, is a Bail Commissioner, within and for the County of Suffolk, duly appointed and qualified as such, and has been actively engaged in taking bail, without the consent of the City Council, and contrary to the provisions of the aforesaid ordinance ; it is hereby

Ordered, That the said Edward J. Jones be and he is hereby removed from the office of Police Commissioner.

Second. The order introduced into the Common Council by Mr. Jesse M. Gove : —

Whereas Section 2 of the ordinances entitled "An ordinance to establish the salaries of the Board of Police Commissioners of the City of Boston," passed on the 14th day of June, 1878, prescribes that the members of said Board of Commissioners shall devote their time to the duties of the office, and shall not actively engage in any other business ; and

Whereas Thomas J. Gargan, one of the members of said Board, has been absent from the City of Boston for more than sixty days ; it is hereby

Ordered, That the said Thomas J. Gargan be and he is hereby removed from the office of Police Commissioner.

Third. The order introduced into the Common Council by Mr. Jesse M. Gove : —

Whereas Section 2 of the ordinance entitled "An ordinance to establish the salaries of the members of the Board of Police Commissioners of the City of Boston," passed on the 14th day of June, 1878, prescribes that the members of said Board shall devote their time to the duties of the office, and shall not actively engage in any other business ; and

Whereas said Police Commissioners are, by virtue of their office, at the head of a department of the City Government whose duty it is to direct and bring before the courts all persons who have violated the criminal laws of the Commonwealth and the ordinances of the city, in order that such persons may be dealt with according to law ; and

Whereas, on the 8th day of June, 1881, Henry Walker, one of said

Police Commissioners, appeared before the Municipal Court of the City of Boston for the transaction of criminal business, as counsel for the defendant in a bastardy process; and

Whereas the said Henry Walker has, while holding the office of Police Commissioner, appeared at various times and in various courts, as counsel in suits pending in said courts, contrary to the provisions of the aforesaid ordinance; it is therefore

Ordered, That Henry Walker be and he hereby is removed from the office of Police Commissioner of the City of Boston.

And, fourth, the communication from Col. Henry Walker, Chairman of the Police Commission, and which communication asked for a full investigation into the official acts of the Commissioners, — beg leave to submit the following

REPORT.

This committee was appointed May 19, 1881, — seven months ago. Their sessions have been over eight in number; they have invited — and some of the members, in their desire to substantiate in some particulars the charges made, have solicited — parties to appear before them to give evidence in relation to matters connected with the Police Commission. After such action; after the drag-net had been cast over the city; after the invitation extended to all who were injured or considered themselves injured by any act of either of the Commissioners, the evidence and the finding of the minority of the committee may be briefly summed up as follows : —

Under the order touching Mr. Jones the evidence submitted to the committee showed that Mr. Jones held at one time the offices of Bail and Insolvency Commissioners and Police Commissioner.

At one of the hearings before the committee Mr. Jones stated, that if it should appear that the holding of the offices of Bail and Insolvency Commissioners interfered with the performance of his duties as Police Commissioner, and thereupon the City Council should advise such action, he would cheerfully resign the offices of Bail and Insolvency Commissioners. By the majority report submitted it appears that all fees earned by Mr. Jones as Bail and Insolvency Commissioners were earned after the hours were given, according to law, to his duties as Police Commissioner.

The minority submitted that no evidence, hearsay or otherwise, was given before the committee showing that Mr. Jones had in any manner or at any time neglected his duties as a Police Commissioner; on the contrary, it appeared that he had endeavored in every way to enforce discipline, and, by visits at all hours to the several police stations, had made himself familiar with the workings of the department.

With such testimony before the committee the undersigned feel that justice to a public officer requires that as far as Mr. Jones is concerned the committee should report that he has in spirit and fact devoted his time to the duties of his office as Police Commissioner.

The reasoning of a majority of the committee, as shown in their report following the statement that "the offices of Police Commissioner and Bail Commissioner are incompatible," presumes that the entire police force of the city is corrupt, and that Police Commissioner Jones was by his acts actively engaged in the endeavor to increase the corruption. In this connection the minority of the committee call attention to the unkind and unchristian-like report of the committee, which charges upon innocent acts of the members of the police force effects which do not and cannot follow, and which charges upon Mr. Jones acts which were not supported by the slightest evidence in the committee.

The minority of the committee further submit that no evidence has been produced by which it can be made to appear that Mr. Jones has in any way neglected the performance of his duties as Police Commissioner.

The question submitted to the City Solicitor in relation to the acts of Mr. Jones was as follows : " Has a Police Commissioner the right under the ordinances, etc., to act as Bail Commissioner or Commissioner of Insolvency, or engage in business of any kind not connected with his office of Police Commissioner, either during office hours or at any other time, for compensation?" The answer of the City Solicitor was as follows : " The ordinance passed June 14, 1878, provides that the members of the Board of Police Commissioners shall devote their time to the duties of the office, and shall not actively engage in any other business." As a fact, showing the unfair spirit in which the majority of the committee have acted, the undersigned refer to the garbled statement made in the majority report, at the close, in which it is stated, in a manner to convey the impression that the Solicitor had given the opinion, " that he (Mr. Jones) could not properly act as Bail Commissioner, Commissioner of Insolvency, and Police Commissioner at the same time," when in fact no such opinion was ever given by the City Solicitor.

To the minority of the committee it seems that Mr. Jones has in no way contravened the intention of the ordinance of June 14, 1878, which was to hinder any member of the Commission from neglecting his duties; and the minority submit that no negligence of police duties has been shown against Mr. Jones. The majority state in their report that the fact that Mr. Jones was a Police Commissioner and a

Bail Commissioner would tend to make a police officer " make as many arrests as possible, in order that his superior officer might get a fee and the subordinate rise in the estimation and good graces of his superior," which is, in effect, that officers would not hesitate to arrest innocent parties, with that end in view, and that Mr. Jones (whose character and reputation need no words of commendation from this committee) would base the promotions in the police force upon the number of bail cases that might be brought to him by officers, — an unfair and unjust statement, which, without evidence of such action on the part of the police officers or Mr. Jones, ought not to be made.

The minority of the committee recommend, therefore, that no action is necessary, and that the order ought not to pass.

WM. WOOLLEY,
JOHN B. FITZPATRICK,
MARTIN T. FOLAN.

Under the order touching Mr. Gargan, the minority of the committee report as follows : That Mr. Gargan appeared before them and made the following statement : that, by reason of overwork, he suffered during the winter months from extreme nervous prostration ; that his physician ordered him to refrain from work and to remove from the city, if he desired to live ; that, after representing to his physician that he desired to go to Mexico, if the climate would agree with him and he might hope to recover his health there, and receiving the answer of his physician that the climate would be favorable to him, he, on the 25th day of March, 1881, left Boston and did not return until June 28, 1881. The evidence before the committee showed that while Mr. Gargan was interested in railroad business, and while in Mexico made some inquiries in relation to railroad matters, he received no compensation for services other than the payment of his expenses.

It appeared in evidence, and uncontradicted, that Mr. Gargan, before leaving Boston, waited upon Mayor Prince, the chief executive officer of the city, submitted to him a physician's certificate stating the fact that he was in ill-health and that it was necessary he should leave Boston for a time, and made an application for leave of absence, and that the Mayor, having on several occasions granted leave of absence to city officials, made a favorable report on the application of Mr. Gargan.

It may be claimed that this evidence, in its entirety, was not presented before the committee ; but it did appear that Mr. Gargan offered to submit his physician's certificate to the inspection of the committee, and to produce Mayor Prince to give testimony as to the fact of the leave of absence being granted.

The majority and minority of the committee both agree that there is no question as to the fact that Mr. Gargan obtained leave of absence from the Mayor ; but the majority claim that under the statute the City Council, and not the Mayor, was the proper body to grant such a leave of absence. And the majority base their claim on the opinion of the City Solicitor, given in answer to the following question :   " Has a Police Commissioner the right under the ordinance to absent himself from the city for a period of thirty days without the consent of the City Council having been first obtained ? " the answer being as follows :   " A Police Commissioner has not the right to absent himself from the city and his duties without the consent of the City Council."

Chapter 244 of the Acts of 1878, being " An act in relation to the Police Department of the City of Boston," states : Section 8.   " The Mayor of the City of Boston shall have the power at all times   .   .   .   to assume command of the whole or any part of the police force in said city," — a provision which, without doubt, gives to the Mayor the virtual control of the entire Police Department.   And while this authority is, perhaps, to be exerted only in case of an emergency, it is evident that the Legislature intended that this power of control over the entire Police Department should exist in the chief executive officer, who is charged with the preservation of order, and who should properly be given such power, and not in a body like the City Council.   Section 1 of the same act gives to the Mayor the power to appoint Police Commissioners and to remove for cause.   Can it be doubted that an authority as broad as that given by this section covers the authority to grant leave of absence ?   But, if it is contended that this may be so, still it is true that, in the past, leave of absence has been granted by the Mayor to heads of departments, and that the precedent has been established for so long and so firmly that both Mr. Gargan in asking for, and the Mayor in granting, leave of absence were fully justified under such circumstances.

In this connection the minority beg leave to refer to the letters " 1 " and " 2 " attached to this report and made a part of it.

The majority of the committee state in their report "that a person who would give any other construction to the statute and ordinances than the one given by the City Solicitor, would be incompetent to perform the duties attendant upon the office of a Police Commissioner of the City of Boston;" and with all due deference to this opinion of the legal gentlemen of the majority of the committee, the minority submit that the statement of His Honor Mayor Prince, that he believed he had such authority, and the further statement contained in the letter marked "**3.**" from Hon. Henry W. Paine, and attached hereto, and which, although not submitted to the committee, is of value as an answer to the opinion of the legal gentlemen of the majority of the committee, and would go far to disprove the statement that, unless a lawyer shall agree with the opinions advanced by the City Solicitor and the legal gentlemen of the majority of the Joint Special Committee on Police Investigation, he is unfit for the position of Police Commissioner.

In the matter of the charge against Mr. Gargan, and the findings of the majority of the committee, the minority refuse to agree, and believe that the desire of the movers in the matter has warped their judgment, and that no action is necessary. The balance of the majority of the committee's report, treating of the nature of punishment to be meted out to offenders, does not seem to the minority of the committee to be properly a part of the duties of an investigating committee.

The minority, therefore, recommend that no action is necessary, and that the order ought not to pass.

> WM. WOOLLEY,
> JOHN B. FITZPATRICK,
> MARTIN T. FOLAN.

Under the order touching Mr. Walker the minority of the committee find nothing to object to,.but rather to commend, in the action of Mr. Walker in the matter of the charge that he appeared as counsel in a bastardy case in the Municipal Court, inasmuch as he had been informed that a grave crime had been committed, and in the furtherance of his duties as a Police Commissioner, he had appeared in the case. The minority of the committee commend Mr. Walker for such action, and also for his action in attending up to the time of trial, without compensation, to cases brought against police officers for acts done in the performance of their duties. No evidence was submitted that he had tried any such cases.

In the matter of the case of James Dorr the following facts appeared : That Dorr was a client of Mr. Walker previous to the appointment of Mr. Walker on the Police Commission ; that, upon his appointment, he gave Mr. Dorr's business into the hands of H. E. Swasey, Esq. ; that Dorr had a civil case pending, which had been tried in the lower court by Mr. Walker, and in which Mr. Dorr had recovered a verdict ; that, when the civil case came up for trial in the Superior Court, Mr. Swasey called upon Mr. Walker and requested him to see the District Attorney, that Mr. Dorr, who had forfeited his bail in a criminal case, might have a safeguard, while in Boston, in attendance on his civil case. Mr. Walker had not acted as counsel for Dorr in the criminal case, and had never acted as counsel for him in any criminal case. Mr. Walker sent a letter to Dorr, whose whereabouts were unknown to him, but directed in care of his (Dorr's) brother, who resided in New York. This letter and the telegram submitted to the committee were only in reference to the civil suit which Mr. Swasey had in charge. The minority submit that these actions of Mr. Walker violated no rule of the Police Department, and were friendly acts toward a former client, having reference only to the conduct of his civil case.

The finding of the majority of the committee, that Mr. Walker knew where Dorr was, is unsupported by the evidence, except so far as the knowledge of the whereabouts of his brother in New York, and the alleged suppression of such information as he had is not borne out by the evidence or the report of the majority of the committee, as it appears that Mr. Walker communicated with the prosecuting officer of the County of Suffolk in relation to Mr. Dorr. No evidence was submitted to disprove the statement of Mr. Walker that he had not acted as counsel for Dorr from the time he became a Police Commissioner.

It appeared in evidence and uncontradicted that Mr. Walker, upon being appointed upon the Police Commission, made an agreement with Hon. E. Gay, who occupied a law office with him, that while he (Walker) was on the Commission no criminal cases should be received in the office, and that Mr. Gay was never directly or indirectly to appear before the commission in any matter, and that the agreement was faithfully carried out. This action of Mr. Walker goes far to contradict any charges that he remained interested in the case of Dorr.

The minority of the committee, therefore, report, that

under the order referred to them, they find no cause to complain of any acts of Mr. Walker enumerated therein or covered by the order; that the acts inquired into were, in the main, such as fell to his duty as a Police Commissioner, and that in the Dorr case he acted honestly, and with no intention to shield Dorr from punishment, and that no action of his therein can be construed into a violation of his duties as a Police Commissioner. Therefore, the minority of the committee report that no action is necessary, and that the order ought not to pass.

WM. WOOLLEY,
M. T. FOLAN,
JOHN B. FITZPATRICK.

Under the communication from Col. Henry Walker, asking for an investigation of the official acts of the Police Commission, the minority report as follows : —

Mr. Walker at all times obeyed the call of the committee to be present at the hearings when required, and showed a willingness to answer all questions which might be asked by the members of the committee in relation to the acts and proceedings of the Commissioner, and showed familiarity with the duties and requirements of his position.

The claim made by the majority report, that three classes of crime quite generally exist in the community, namely, the illegal sale of liquor, gambling, and the keeping of houses of ill-fame, cannot be well doubted, and the fact is evident also that such evils have heretofore existed, and, in the judgment of the minority of the committee, are likely still to exist in such a large city as Boston.

Under the former Commission, when Col. Russell was chairman, these crimes were quite general, and if the number of gambling-houses, houses of ill-fame, and stores where liquor is illegally sold, has not decreased since then, it is evident that it has not increased.

It is claimed in the majority report that Mr. Walker, in answer to inquiry made by one of the committee, stated that he did not know what the common report in relation to certain houses in a street in this city was. A careful reading of the evidence will show that the statement made by him was, that he did not have such evidence as would convict parties of keeping such places in violation of law.

The statement of the citizen who came before the committee was, in effect, that he spoke to Mr. Walker in relation to the locality in which he (the citizen) lived, and complained of the neighborhood; that this interview took place upon the street; that Mr. Walker desired him, if he wished to speak upon police business, to call at the Police Commissioners' office; and at the office, on another occasion, Mr. Walker informed him that the matter would be inquired into; that time was necessary to perform the duty, etc. The citizen further stated that the neighborhood had been improved in some respects; and as to this matter the minority of the committee believe that Mr. Walker and the other Commissioners have not been remiss in the performance of their duties.

It is true that all men who believe that they have been treated discourteously magnify the ill-treatment that they believe they have received; and it is submitted that, while every public officer should treat applicants for information and complaints courteously, the person who feels himself aggrieved is not always a fair witness and likely to give impartial testimony. It should be remembered that this testimony was given in the absence of Mr. Walker, and that he has had no opportunity to admit or deny the allegations. In relation to the matter of the hearing of the complaint on the action of certain police officers at Sharon, it appeared that it became necessary to summon different members of the police force before the Commissioners for identification, and that the complainant, chafing at the necessary delay, refused to proceed further, claiming that the witnesses could not be brought to appear.

The minority desire to place in a proper light the answers of Mr. Walker to questions asked him, and from which answers the majority undertake to draw conclusions showing that the chairman of the Police Commission was unfamiliar with his duties. Whenever Mr. Walker was interrogated in relation to events, figures, dates, and facts, some of them two years old, while declining to put himself upon the record except by general answers, he at all times invited the committee to examine the records of the Commissioners, and expressed a perfect readiness to furnish such information from the books of the Commission.

In relation to the matter of granting licenses the minority can remember no proper evidence submitted which showed any unfairness in the matter. The question of the granting of the license to the Briggs House, and whether the Commissioners have exceeded their powers, is now before the courts, and presumably will be decided in favor of the Commissioners; and to the minority of the committee a charge that the Commissioners had failed in their duty would be ill-timed and ill-advised in view of these circumstances, and in the event of a decision supporting the action of the Commissioners there might be reason to doubt the judgment on law questions of the majority of the committee.

As to the sales of liquor between the hours of 12 and 6 A.M., and on Sundays, a careful reading of the testimony will show that the evidence was, that certain places were open between such hours and on Sundays. All hotels are by law allowed to remain open; and while it is true, no doubt, that liquor can be purchased at such times, still evidence of violation of law sufficient to convict offenders cannot always be had.

While the committee have heard a mass of evidence, the greater part of which would not be admitted in any court of justice in the country; while men who have had requests refused, men who have hobbies, men whose licenses have been rejected, and, in fact, men who had any grievance against the Commissioners, have been permitted to testify as to acts, conversations with third persons, and matters which could not be properly admitted, the minority believe that after seven months' careful hearing nothing has been found to warrant any complaint against the chairman or either member of the Commission.

The orders originally introduced by a member of the Council were based upon evidence already submitted to the gentleman; and it is fair to say that his action in the matter must have been, and would likely continue throughout the hearing to be, prejudiced against the members of the Commission whose acts he was to judge.

To the members of the City Council it is only necessary to call attention to the majority report of the findings of the committee, and to the recommendations, to make it apparent that no evidence has been submitted which calls for the recommendations, and that, taking into account the time spent and the thoroughness of the investigation, the Commissioners are to be commended that so little which, in any manner, is discreditable to them, should be shown.

The minority of the committee believe that the chairman of the Police Commission has shown due diligence in the performance of his duties, and a full knowledge of the requirements of his position. And the undersigned, dissenting from the report of the committee, recommend that no action is necessary.

The minority join in the recommendation of the majority in relation to the separation of the duties of Police and License Commissioners.

WM. WOOLLEY,
JOHN B. FITZPATRICK,
MARTIN T. FOLAN.

[**1.**]

48 POPLAR STREET, BOSTON,
Wednesday Evening, Dec. 21, 1881.

To His Honor the Mayor: —

DEAR SIR, — Will you please inform me as a member of the Joint Special Committee on Investigation of Police Commisssioners what has been the practice as to granting leave of absence to commissioners and heads of departments? If application was made by Police Commissioner Thos. J. Gargan for leave of absence, and if you granted such leave of absence?

Yours very truly,

JOHN B. FITZPATRICK.

[**2.**]

JOHN B. FITZPATRICK, ESQ. : —

Dear Sir, — On several occasions applications have been made to me by city officials for leave of absence, which have been granted, although I do not find any law giving me authority in such cases. Understanding that it was customary for the executive to exercise such powers I assumed that there was propriety in doing so.

Mr. Gargan asked permission to be absent at the time referred to by you, and I complied with his request, as he was ill.

FREDERICK O. PRINCE.

[**3.**

BOSTON, Dec. 22, 1881.

MY DEAR SIR: — I understand that your medical adviser deemed it necessary for the recovery of your health that you should go abroad; that as a member of the Board of Police Commissioners you applied to the Mayor for leave of absence, obtained it, and went to Mexico.

I cannot doubt that you were right in applying to the Mayor, or that he was authorized to grant your request.

Very truly yours,

H. W. PAINE.

THOMAS GARGAN, ESQ.

APPENDIX.

INVESTIGATION OF POLICE COMMISSIONERS.

Seventh Hearing.

FRIDAY, Dec. 2, 1881.

The committee met at 11 o'clock, A.M. Present, Aldermen VILES (Chairman) and HERSEY, and Councilmen GOVE, HART, and FITZPATRICK.

Mr. HART. — Mr. Crosby comes here, this morning, to give us a little information in reference to the licensing of the Briggs House, located next to the Children's Mission on Tremont street. I think that introduction is all that will be necessary.

The CHAIRMAN. — Well, Mr. Hart, if you know the facts, the committee are willing you should bring them out.

Mr. HART. — I think Mr. Crosby can tell us the facts better than I can bring them out in any other way.

Mr. CROSBY. — Shall I tell you the whole story?

The CHAIRMAN. — You might as well begin at the beginning.

STATEMENT OF MR. WILLIAM CROSBY.

The Children's Mission for the Destitute, — you may, perhaps, not know about it, — the theory is, that it is carried on by children; it has been in existence thirty-three years — to help orphan and destitute children; first, those in the City of Boston, and then those coming from other places. It takes them and provides homes in the country for them; and has taken out of your city something over six thousand, who have been placed about, saving you a great expense. If we had not taken care of them they would have been in your institutions. Next door to us is the Briggs House, a place — as we understood, and have understood for years — of very bad repute, resorted to by young people, and which bears a very bad character. Something more than two years ago my attention was called to it by one of the liquor squad, — I think one of the police who had charge of licenses, — who asked me if I knew the character of it, supposing I would object to the granting of a license for it. I did then send in an objection to the Commissioners; but no attention was paid to it.

The CHAIRMAN. — That was before the present law was passed?

Mr. CROSBY. — Yes, sir.

The CHAIRMAN. — Now the law is, that if a person object, they cannot grant a license.

Mr. CROSBY. — At our regular meeting, in June, I called the attention of our committee to that; and it seemed a very simple thing to do. All we had to do was to object. We made that objection; but heard nothing of it until the 25th of July. On that day Major Mahan called to see me. He came on the part of Mr. Garvey.

The CHAIRMAN. — Is that the proprietor of the house?

Mr. CROSBY. — He is the proprietor. They had found that we objected to granting the license, and were surprised at it, as the house was kept in a very orderly manner; there was nothing objectionable about it; it had been approved of by Col. Russell, Mr. Whitmore, and others; that Mr. Garvey was a wounded soldier, and that he had invested a good deal of money there. I told him that places of this kind were the very cause of our being where we were, and doing this work; that at the time we were taking care of the children of drunkards, if we did not object, we were virtually saying to these men, "You may spend your money at the Briggs House, and we will take care of your children"; that he could not expect us to do that, and that we could not withdraw the objection. He said that Mr. Garvey would change the character of his business; that he would give up his bar. I told him that nothing short of an agreement that not a drop of liquor should be sold on the premises would induce us to withdraw our objection. He went away. The next notice I had was on the 11th of August, when a police officer wanted me to come to the Police Commissioners' office as quickly as I could. There I found Mr. Garvey, Major Mahan, and one or two witnesses. They were going to have a hearing. I stated that it was not at all proper to have a hearing without giving me notice; I did not know why I was sent for, and, of course, was unprepared. The commissioners saw it was not proper, and appointed the 16th of August for the hearing. Major Mahan had stated, in the first place, that we did not adjoin. The estate next us was owned by Charles W. Galloupe at the time Mr. Garvey had his lease, and has since been sold to a man by the name of Dearborn, and is all one estate. Next to us is a small building with fifteen or twenty feet front, occupied by a Chinese laundry; that being between us, Major Mahan said we did not join, and, therefore, could not object. But he saw, when I called his attention to it, that right in the rear of this Chinese laundry is a wooden building of three stories, I think, — two and a half or three stories, — built up against our wall, which is connected with the Briggs House by a gallery, and occupied by them; in the rear, another building, built up against ours, which is used by them. The whole estate, with the exception of the ground on which this little Chinese laundry stands, is all occupied by the Briggs House; so I think he had to withdraw that objecton. That was the objection which we supposed we should have to meet at our first meeting, and I then employed Mr. Ellis L. Motte, one of our committee, who is a lawyer, as our counsel, to attend this meeting with me. We took no witnesses then, because we supposed the whole ques-

tion would be whether we joined or not, and that we were prepared
to prove. But, at that meeting, Major Mahan said, that their petition was for a license as an innholder ; that the law allowed us to
object to the granting of a license to a common victualler, but not
to an innholder ; we stated that he was not an innholder ; that if he
had a license for one, it was only an evasion of the law ; that he
did not in any sense keep a hotel.

The CHAIRMAN. — An innholder is a hotel-keeper. The Parker
House requires an innholder's license.

Mr. CROSBY. — This hotel has a few rooms, which, perhaps,
accommodate a few lodgers ; but it is not a hotel in any sense of
the word. No carriage was ever seen to drive up there and leave
a person with baggage. They brought, as witnesses, a gentleman
who said that he was a travelling salesman, who lived in Roxbury,
and who was in the habit of stopping there and eating his lunch before going home ; another man, who lived on Hollis street, near by,
who said he went in there, although he did not drink anything ;
and one or two policemen. One of the policemen was asked
whether he would take his wife or his children there, and he stated
that he should prefer to go to some place where liquor was not
so openly sold. He was asked if he had ever seen any person
stop there, and he said he had, — some persons who arrived late at
night. That was the amount of the testimony they had ; but nothing to show that it was a hotel. We had no witnesses at that
meeting. The meeting was rather a long one, and it was ad-
journed to the 20th. We then brought, as witnesses, Mr. Gay,
who lives directly opposite, on the corner of Hollis street ; Mr.
Swan, who is the principal of the Winthrop School ; Capt. Adams,
the Superintendent of Police ; another man, who had been in the
habit of going in there, and who stated that he had been accosted
there by women ; and another man, a Mr. Lawrence, who had
been in there to get lunch or something, and while sitting in one of
the stalls had heard obscene and profane language between young
men and women there ; Sergeant Thomas of the station in La
Grange street, and two or three police officers. The neighbors around there have been afraid to do or say anything in
the way of making a complaint. It has been a great nuisance
to all the neighborhood, on account of the condition of things on
the sidewalk, but to Mr. Gay, more than to others, because, at
night, even as late as two or three o'clock, he had been disturbed
by the Briggs House turning their customers out at that time,
when they were shutting up for the night ; and on Sundays, by a
continual going in and out there. Mr. Swan, the principal of the
school, stated, that though he did not know anything about that
particular house, the places of that kind were a cause of great
trouble to him on account of his girls. He said that often people
about these places spotted the girls, got acquainted with them,
and at times he had some difficulty in keeping them straight. He
has some six or seven hundred of them. He said that no place of
that kind should be licensed in the vicinity of a school for girls or
boys, or in the vicinity of an institution like ours. The Superin-

tendent of Police testified to the bad character of it, and to what he had seen. He told me privately it was not a hotel. Said he, "That is not a hotel; it is nothing but a drinking saloon." He objected strongly to the licensing of such a place in the vicinity of the Winthrop School, or in the vicinity of our institution. At our place there are children all the time during the day. On Sundays there is Sunday school and Sunday service; on Tuesday evening and Thursday evening there are meetings, and at the same time that our young people are going in there they see other young people going into the Briggs House to drink. We had a long session. I wanted to prove that day the character of the house by an occurrence which took place there on the 17th of March, about two years before. Upon inquiry at the station at La Grange street, I found that the character of the house was bad; it was well known to all the police to be bad. They told me of a man who was arrested there on the morning of the 17th in company with a woman not his wife. The result was that he was brought up before the Municipal Court and got off by the payment of a considerable fine, and the husband of the woman got a divorce. I found the detective who had spotted this man — he did not arrest him — and I wanted him to appear before the commissioners. But it is impossible to get any one to appear willingly, and we had no power to force an appearance. Even the police officers, several of them, begged me not to call them into the case. They all dislike it very much; but you probably know that better than I can tell you.

The CHAIRMAN. — The same experience we have had here all through.

Mr. CROSBY. — Notwithstanding that there were two or three who did come. This detective said, "You don't want me; you have the records of the Municipal Court; ask the commissioners to procure them, and the clerk will produce them." I wrote a letter to them asking them to summon this officer, and the clerk of the court, and to ask the clerk to bring his records of that day. At this meeting I inquired if they were there, and they said, "No." By the way, they refused to allow us to put that in, "because," they said, "it is so far back. We will restrict this to whatever evidence you can bring in regard to what has happened within one year." I wanted to bring that in.

The CHAIRMAN. — How long has Mr. Garvey occupied this house, one or two years?

Mr. CROSBY. — Oh, yes, sir, several years. It is four or five years; I don't remember exactly. I wanted to prove that this man who went into Mr. Garvey's lived not far from him; had been in business a good while; doing a large business; was well known to Mr. Garvey; and that he must have known when this man came there that he was not a proper person. But that we could not show. The commissioners said, "No matter about that; we know all about it, and it is too far back." As they knew all about it, I thought that was sufficient. I think I have told you pretty much the amount of the testimony these people gave. It was all against its being a hotel, and showing that it was a place frequented by young people, and people of bad character. I heard nothing more until the 5th of September. Mr. Garvey sent one of his personal friends to me, who went through the same course of reasoning that Mr. Garvey did. On the 5th of September, as I was going home at night, some one beckoned to me from a street car. I jumped on, and it was Major Jones. He said, "Mr. Crosby, we have utterly refused to give that man a license." Said I, "I am glad to hear it; but, Major, how long can he go on selling?" Said he, "I don't think he is selling now." I said, "I think he is. How long do you give them?" He replied, "We generally give them four or five days, and then we usually close them up." As I understood him, he should close him up. On the 8th, about that time, while this was going on, some one sent me a copy of the "Sunday Mail," in which was a notice of the Briggs House, stating that the front door was closed, but that on Sunday it was easy to get access there, as usual. And in the same paper was an account of the proceedings before the Police Commissioners, and a statement something like this: That where a person failed to obtain a license, if he applied to Mr. Jenkins, who had an office at 61 Court street, gave him a fee of $25 and paid some other expenses, he was pretty sure to get his license. On the 8th of September Mr. Garvey came in to see me, and with him a gentleman who introduced himself as Mr. Jenkins, one of Mr. Garvey's counsel. He went through the same persuasive course of reasoning that Major Mahan did: It was a very nice place. Mr. Garvey was a wounded soldier trying hard to get a living. It was too bad to interfere with him, and we had better not do it. If we let him alone, and he made money, perhaps, by and by, he would give our institution some money. I told Mr. Garvey we should be very glad to have him keep his money; but we did not wish to have him use it in such a disreputable way; or, at any rate, not near us; we would prefer his absence to his money. He said that Mr. Garvey was willing to make any change in his business that would be satisfactory to us. He would give up the bar, and would see that nothing disreputable was carried on. I have the records of that meeting, because I put it down at that time, and I will just read to you what I wrote: —

"This afternoon Mr. P. A. Garvey, of the Briggs House, called, with a friend, who introduced himself as Mr. Jenkins, one of Mr. Garvey's counsel. Mr. J. said that they had called to see whether they could not remove our objections, in order that Mr. Garvey might continue his business. Whether, if he closed earlier, and sold no liquor on Sundays, and allowed nothing improper or objectionable in the conduct of those who visited the place, we would be satisfied, and withdraw our objections. I answered that the only way to satisfy us would be to give up the sale of liquor entirely. I stated to them what our work is: that the suffering we are obliged to relieve is caused, in the great majority of cases, by such saloons as his; that we are continually obliged to take charge of, and support the children of, parents who could support them, but who spend their earnings in such places ; that we consider it wrong to do so, and not do all in our power to prevent it ; that it is our duty to put an end to the cause whenever we can ; that it would be wrong for us to allow such a place near our Mission without protesting against it. Mr. Garvey stated that he was a man in poor health ; was wounded in the late war, his constitution injured, and was unable to do much work ; that his expenses were large, as he was obliged to keep *seven* persons in his employ ; that he kept a horse, as his physician recommended him to ride a great deal. (All this seemed to prove that he must make a great deal of money.) He said, further, that he did not sell to people who were drunk ; that customers often would not take meals that were being cooked for them if they could not have their drinks with them ; that in a place like his they could not prevent a certain class of girls from frequenting there, though when there they were required to be orderly. To this I replied that he had given one of the strongest reasons that could be given why such a place should not be open in the vicinity of a church, an institution for children, or a school for girls. After a full statement upon both sides, all of which was said in a perfectly pleasant and gentlemanly manner, the parties left. Mr. C. told them he had no enmity against Mr. Garvey, but considered it to be his duty to do all in his power to prevent any such business from being carried on in the vicinity of the Mission."

The CHAIRMAN. — This was at your place?

Mr. CROSBY. — They called on me at the office of the Mission. That was on the 8th of September. Well, nothing was heard after that until the 13th. On the 13th I was sent for to go to the office of the Police Commissioners. I went there and found Major Jones. He called in, at the same time that he called me in, this Mr. Jenkins. He said, " Mr. Crosby, did you see any difference in the Briggs House on Sunday?" I said, " No ; I am not there Sundays." — " Well," said he, " I think they do not sell on Sundays." The moment I left his office I met a gentleman who said he saw a girl seated at a table in an upper room, and he saw one of the waiters bring liquor to her ; so they did sell liquor on Sunday. Major Jones handed me then the document which I had sent in — the objection which I had sent in by direction of the committee. He handed that to me and said, " Mr. Crosby, we are told that there was no vote of the committee authorizing this objection ; that it is a personal matter of your own ; that the committee passed no such vote." I said, " Major, this reads that at a meeting of our committee I was instructed to do so and so. Do you mean that when I wrote that I wrote a falsehood?" He replied, " No, no, Mr. Crosby, we do not mean to say exactly that ; but we are told so." Said I, " If you are told so it is by some person who knows or who professes to know." Said he, " It is John Mason Everett." I said, " Mr. Everett is one of our committee ; but he was not at this meeting." Then he turned to Mr. Jenkins and said, " I suppose, Mr. Jenkins, there is no reason why we should not tell Mr. Crosby the whole story, or all about it?" Mr. Jenkins said, " No." Then he said, " Mr. Whitmore tells us that he has seen Mr. Everett, and Mr. Everett tells him that he was not present; but he was informed by one of the committee present that there was no such vote passed." Said I, " Do you remember that Mr. Motte, who is one of our corporation, and one of our committee, told you that the committee did pass such a vote, and that it was no act of mine, but was the act of the committee?" Said he, " I do; I had forgotten it." We then had considerable conversation about this matter of his selling. Said I, " Major, how long can he go on without a license? He sold from the first of May to the 23d of September without a license. He was refused a license on the 17th or 19th of July — somewhere along there; he was then refused a license after two hearings; and still the commissioners allowed him to go on without a license up to the 23d of September." Major Jones said, " I don't think he is selling. Mr. Garvey and his friends there say that he is not." Said I, " Major, I saw the other day so many barrels of beer left at his place and empty barrels taken away. On such another day I saw so many more barrels left there. Now, don't you suppose if liquor was left there, he sold it?" Said he, " I suppose he did." After leaving Major Jones' office I went immediately to Mr. Everett, and without telling him my business I said, " Do you know Mr. Whitmore?" He said, " Yes; he is a neighbor of mine."—" He has been to see you," I said, " what did he say?" Mr. Everett replied, " He said he was surprised to find we objected to the licensing of the Briggs House; that Mr. Garvey was a wounded soldier, and he had a good deal of sympathy for him, and he hoped we would withdraw the objection. His house was well conducted."

Mr. Everett said that Mr. Whitmore hoped we would not object, and said he supposed it was a personal matter with Mr. Crosby. Said I, " What did you say to him?" — " Well," Mr. Everett said, " I said that the date of that objection was the time for the regular meeting of the committee, and if you were authorized you were probably authorized at that meeting; and if I had been there I should have voted for it, for it was the proper thing to do." And out of that the story was reported to the commissioners that I was not authorized, and that there was no such vote. There was one matter at the first meeting that I had forgotten, and that I want to speak about. Major Mahan, when he claimed that this was a hotel, was asked whether they kept a hotel register. He said they did. He made answer for his witness. Mr. Garvey was on the stand, and the Major answered for him. " Will you produce it?"— "At the next meeting." The commissioners were asked to require that hotel register they were now keeping, and as far back as it could be, produced. It was called for at the second hearing. It was not there, but they said it would be there in a few moments. When it came in it was an entirely new book that had been just bought. It was commenced on the 16th of August, the day of our first hearing, and it was arranged as no hotel register ever was seen to be arranged, that is, it was headed August 16th, and at the middle of the page August 17th, and so on, giving half a page for each day. The first entry in it was some one for supper; after that some one for dinner; and the whole thing showed that it was manufactured for the occasion. The Major was ashamed of it, and said, " We have another."— " Well, where is it?"— " It is in Peter Low's bindery." Peter Low's bindery! That seemed very strange that a book of so little value should be sent to a bindery. " Yes," said he, " Peter Low sent his boy to my office to take it to the bindery." Well, then, it seemed very queer that the hotel register of the Briggs House should be at a lawyer's office on Court street. It occured to me that Peter Low was dead. I did not say anything about it, because I did not know but possibly he had left a son. But I found that the name appeared the last time in the directory in 1873, and he was then working at the Boston Public Library, and had no bindery of his own. I went to the Library, and they told me that he had no bindery of his own for three years, but that he worked there then. I inquired why he had no bindery, as I had known him when I was in the book business. " Why," they said, " he was intemperate, and let his business all run away from him." Said I, " When did he die?" They could not give me the exact date, but I went to the Registrar's office, and found that it was on the 22d of December, 1874. For seven years he had been dead, and for ten years he had had no bindery. And yet Major Mahan said that book was taken by his boy to his bindery. I wrote to the commissioners, made that statement, and told them where they could verify these facts if they chose to. It was on the 13th that I had my interview with Major Jones and Mr. Jenkins. On the 17th I went into the country on vacation, and was gone three weeks. The regular meeting of the committee was deferred until my return, which was on the 8th of October, of a Saturday. At that meeting Mr. Everett was present, and I stated to the committee the whole story pretty much as I have stated it to you. I asked Mr. Everett to correct me in regard to his interview, and he said that I stated it correctly. But he said, " Mr. Whitmore don't care anything about it now; Mr. Garvey has got his license." I said, " He has not. The commissionners assured me that they had positively refused it." Mr. Everett said, " Well, probably Mr. Whitmore knows as much about it as you, as he is in the ring. If he says so, he probably has got it." I went, after the meeting, to the commissioners' office, and it was closed. I went then to the station on La Grange street, and they told me he was licensed on the 23d of September.

Mr. GOVE. — What was this date when they told you he had been refused?

Mr. CROSBY. — When they told me it had been refused was on the 5th of September. After that, on the 15th of September, I met Major Jones, and then the license had not been granted, and Mr. Jenkins was arguing his case for him, trying to bring it about. On the 10th of October, I think it was, the next Monday, I called on Mr. Motte, our lawyer. We went to the Police Commissioners, and Mr. Motte said, " We have come to inquire the result of the hearing; we have heard nothing officially." Mr. Gargan, who seems to have been the spokesman through the whole of this, and who has had more to say than any of the others, said, " Well, we concluded, after hearing the testimony, that he was not entitled to a license as an innholder, and we thought, as a sort of compromise, as Mr. Crosby's objection was to his selling liquor on Sunday and keeping open late at night, that we would give him a license as a common victualler, and we then could look after him and see that everything was carried on properly." I said, " Mr. Gargan, my objection was not that he kept open Sunday, or that he kept open late at night ; my objection was to his having any license to sell liquor at all, and you have no right to think that any compromise will be satisfactory, certainly, without asking us."

Mr. HERSEY. — Does the same statute apply in regard to an adjoining estate in both cases ? Are they obliged to refuse in both cases if the owner of an adjoining estate objects ?

Mr. CROSBY. — The statute mentions a common victualler ; it does not mention an innholder. The ground Major Mahan took was that we had no right to object, their license being for an innholder.

Mr. HERSEY. — That is where you thought the statute would shut him out ?

Mr. CROSBY. — We proved to the satisfaction of the commissioners that he was not an innholder, and was not entitled to an innholder's license. Now they turn around and offer him a license as a common victualler, which he did not want. I asked Mr. Gargan, " Why do you give him a license that he does not ask for ? " He replied : " Well, we had sympathy for the man, and we thought this would be satisfactory all round." I told him they had no right to suppose it would be satisfactory. Then Mr. Motte asked whether they had any hearing, and he said, " No." He asked whether it was proper to grant a license without a hearing. " Well," he said, " they had authority to open a case whenever they pleased, and to do as they pleased about it." We then asked whether this was advertised in a proper manner if a common victualler's license was wanted. In the first place I asked him why he should grant it when it was not wanted, and his reply was : " As the greater includes the less, and as he asked for a license as an innholder, Class A, we had a right to give him anything in that class that we chose." I said, " Why give him something that he did not want, because we could object to it ?" Well, there was no particularly satisfactory reply given to that. Then he was asked : " Was this advertised, and should it not have been advertised as a new application ?" Well, he thought it should. He turned to Major Jones, and said, " Was this advertised ?" Major Jones replied, " I think not." While we were talking their clerk brought in two blanks, which were filled out in a hurry. One of them was dated October, and a finger drawn through it to erase it ; and then it was dated May 1st. It was an application for a license as a common victualler, dated May 1st, twenty-three or twenty-four days before their application for a license as an innholder. It was not certified to, or the names of five or six citizens that are required to back up his application were not upon it. It was not in due form, and evidently was made on the spot, and dated back, in order that it might appear that he had applied for a license as a common victualler. Major Jones took that, and on the back indorsed, I think, " Received October 13," if I recollect. At any rate, the papers are in the office.

Mr. HERSEY. — Indorsed while you were there?

Mr. CROSBY. — While I was there. Said he, " I have to indorse on this paper the day it was received."

The CHAIRMAN. — Who brought that in?

Mr. CROSBY. — It was brought in by their clerk.

The CHAIRMAN. — Did they send for it?

Mr. CROSBY. — They did not send for it.

Mr. GOVE. — This was the only case you were there to object to?

Mr. CROSBY. — Yes, sir.

Mr. GOVE. — And it was well known that you were there to object to the Briggs House?

Mr. CROSBY. — Certainly ; of course.

Mr. HERSEY. — Did this have the appearance of being freshly made ; was the ink dry?

Mr. CROSBY. — I should say it was in pencil. I should say that " October " was written in ink and a finger drawn across it ; but, if I recollect, it was filled out in pencil.

Mr. FITZPATRICK. — Was this an application that you speak of ?

Mr. CROSBY. — It was a pretended application for a license as common victualler. It was dated twenty-three or twenty-four days before his application for a license as an innholder ; and he did not want a common victualler's license.

Mr. FITZPATRICK. — Previous to this year he has had an innholder's license?

Mr. CROSBY. — Yes, sir.

Mr. FITZPATRICK. — Since it has been granted has he done the same kind of business?

Mr. CROSBY. — I think he has.

Mr. FITZPATRICK. — Does he keep his place open publicly on Sunday?

Mr. CROSBY. — Not publicly. I do not think his front door has been wide open, but it has been open so that any one could get in.

Mr. FITZPATRICK. — It has not been open so publicly as when he had an innholder's license?

Mr. CROSBY. — No, I should say that the entrance to the ladies' saloon has been open ; I should say that now it was closed, but that any one could open it.

Mr. GOVE. — Well, there never was any change until this piece came out in the " Mail" ; then, immediately afterward, was there apparent cessation of business?

Mr. CROSBY. — No change then.

Mr. HERSEY. — What was the date of the piece in the " Mail"?

Mr. CROSBY. — I do not remember the date.

Mr. GOVE. — If I remember it was some time about the first of September.

Mr. CROSBY. — Well, Mr. Gargan was asked : " Supposing it

was not advertised, as we think it was not, if it did not go through the legal form, is he legally licensed?" Mr. Gargan said, "No. If it was not advertised, that license is void." — "Well, will you send for the papers and see whether it is or not?" They sent out for the clerk, but the clerk was on a vacation, and they came back. "Well, the clerk has gone, and among these three thousand papers we cannot find it; but in a few days we will find out and tell you." So in two or three days we went again. Mr. Gargan said, "We notified Garvey to stop selling, and immediately his counsel called and called our attention to a little word *or* in the law, which he says alters the whole case. The law provides that the applicant shall state the character *or* class of license that he wants. Now, he says they claim that, under that clause, we have the right to grant any license 'of any character under that class; and we must refer that to the City Solicitor." Well, we asked whether they would do it, and do it at once, and they said they would. A few days afterwards I received this notice from them.

[The notice was handed to the chairman, who read it, as follows : —]

BOSTON, Oct. 18, 1881.

WILLIAM CROSBY, ESQ., *Supt. Children's Mission, Tremont street :* —

Dear Sir, — The commissioners have consulted the City Solicitor in regard to the publication of the license of Peter A. Garvey, Tremont street, and he has decided that the publication, as it had been done in this case, is a sufficient and legal one.

Yours respectfully,
F. C. GOLDTHWAIT,
Clerk.

Mr. HERSEY. — What question did they propose to the City Solicitor?

Mr. CROSBY. — I don't know. I suppose it was the question of advertisement. But that does not authorize them to grant a license as common victualler, when the law says it shall not be granted if objection is made ; it does not cover that at all.

Mr. HERSEY. — The question that was asked the City Solicitor might have been on the application for a license by this Garvey, published so and so — "Is that sufficient notice?" They may not have put the whole question. That is the point, — whether it was sufficient notice to warrant giving him a license as a common victualler.

Mr. CROSBY. — But it is a very singular state of things if, when a man asks for one thing, they can give him another that he does not ask for.

Mr. HERSEY. — It seems to me they would have the right to do that, no party objecting. But that is your objection. No, it don't seem to me that they would, on the whole, because you know that your objection would not avail as against an innholder, but would as against a common victualler. You ought to have notice where your objection could be made valid. It shuts out the man who might put his objection in, in one case, and, in the other case, it would be open to him. Of course, the intention would be that you should have notice of a particular application.

Mr. CROSBY. — I called on Mr. Motte. Before I had time to say anything about this — by the way, Mr. Motte had told me that he had some business with the City Solicitor, and he should ask him himself about this matter — before I had time to say anything about this, he said, "I have seen the City Solicitor, and he says these men were not right in granting the license." I then handed him this paper. Said he, "It is very strange. I am going to see him again at twelve o'clock." At two o'clock he saw him; and he told him that he had given the commissioners this opinion; that he had advised them so after looking more thoroughly into the law. Of course, what the question was I do not know. I then went to the commissioners, and they told me that they had the right, under the first application, to grant any license in the first class, and that, therefore, they wrote it in. I told them that, taking their own statement that the greater included the less, and that in the application the license under the head First Class, A, was included, they had already refused him a license in July; and, again, after repeated hearings, refused him a common victualler's license; and that after such refusal he was not any longer an applicant under that advertisement; but if he could apply for one, must apply again, and the application should be advertised. They said they had the right to open a case and grant a license without any hearing. That is, I believe, the whole of the matter.

Mr. GOVE. — Your Children's Mission is a corporation, is it not?

Mr. CROSBY. — Yes, sir.

Mr. GOVE. — And the fee to this estate rests in the corporation?

Mr. CROSBY. — Yes, sir.

Mr. GOVE. — Now, will you just step here, please. Here, you see, is a plan of the estates there. As I understand it, that place there is occupied by a Chinese laundry?

Mr. CROSBY. — Yes, sir.

Mr. HERSEY. — They run right round it, I presume.

Mr. GOVE. — Yes.

Mr. CROSBY. — The Chinese told me that they have no right in the way at all. They have nothing except that building and the ground it stands on. I won't be very sure about that. But I have pursued this a little farther. This stands in the name of Charles W. Galloupe. I find he has sold it to J. Henry Dearborn. Mr. Garvey, in the first place, hired this, wherever the Briggs House is, and this yard about it, and the shed attached to it there. It then consisted of three tenements. There was a store, and there were two stories above. He has altered it, and made it into one, and has hired these additional buildings; and, also, since his lease from Mr. Galloupe, since Mr. Dearborn bought it, he has hired all the rest of Mr. Dearborn. There is a gallery, which extends to that building. The proportions here are not correct. That, I think, should be smaller; this should extend to the Briggs House, and there is a gallery extending across from here to that building. The general idea of it is right.

Mr. GOVE. — So that the Briggs House is connected with the Mission here?

Mr. CROSBY. — Yes, sir. Even if it was not, all this is one estate, and he hires all the rest. There is no question but that he joins.

Mr. HERSEY. — Their theory in granting this license was, they assumed that you did not object. They must have assumed that.

Mr. CROSBY. — No ; they could not have assumed it.

Mr. HERSEY. — They must have assumed that, because, otherwise, the statute would compel them to refuse the license. Are they not bound by statute?

Mr. CROSBY. — No, sir.

Mr. HERSEY. — Are they not?

Mr. CROSBY. — No, sir. Well, they don't go as far as that. They paid no sort of attention to this. Now, our attention has been called to another thing. This man has been violating the screen law. As you pass by his place you cannot see any selling going on in the building. He has an office in the front of the building which takes in the whole of the front window. He has there a safe. There is a glass door in that office, but you cannot see anything that is going on in his saloon. His front door has been a door covered with morocco leather, which you cannot see anything through. Yesterday he took that door down, and has put up a double glass door, which is made either of hammered or ground glass ; and you cannot see anything through that. In the room overhead, called the ladies' saloon, he has window shades, which draw up from the bottom, and as soon as it is dark these are drawn up. Inside are these stalls which you find in oyster saloons. Now, I say he has no right to have these stalls, where these young men and women can go in — and I have seen them go in, and seen liquor carried to them — and you cannot see. He has no right to have any obstruction ; for the law is so explicit that not even a mosquito net is allowable, if it obstructs the view. No exhibition of bottles is allowed in the windows, or anything to prevent a clear view.

Mr. HERSEY. — If they claim that they granted this on his old application for an innholder's license, that the greater included the less, and that, therefore, that was an application for either, you having made objections to him as an innholder, why, under the same ruling, would not your objection cover anything that was less than that? I do not see how they got around the objection of the adjoining estate.

Mr. GOVE. — He put it into his objection. He has said, " We objected to his receiving a license as an innholder, and not as a common victualler."

Mr. CROSBY. — We did not object to it as anything ; we objected to his license.

Mr. HERSEY. — That covered whatever they might construe his application to be for.

Mr. CROSBY. — I asked Mr. Gargan this at this last interview. I said, "Why did you give him a license that he does not ask for, — one that he said we could object to?" — "Well," he says, "there were so many people who came here to plead for him, and we had such sympathy for the man, and we thought it was a fair way to compromise it." He said, as I thought first, "More than five hundred people came here to speak or to interview us for him." I called his attention to it, and said, "You say five hundred people?" — "Well, no ; not so many." — "How many do you say?" —"Well, three or four hundred." —"Then you acknowledge that you allowed your sympathy to lead you to give this kind of a license against your better judgment? You have had these hearings ; you have heard all sides, and you are satisfied he is not entitled to it, and now your sympathy leads you to grant it?" Said I, "You have no sympathy for those six or seven hundred girls who Mr. Swan told you were in such danger. You thought nothing of the Superintendent of Police, who gave you his opinion about licensing such a place in the vicinity of ours. You thought nothing of an institution carried on by such men as Henry P. Kidder and Mr. Faulkner, and others, who are an honor to the city, contributing their money to every benevolent work carried on in your city ; nor for this place of ours, which is saving thousands of dollars to the city every year, not requiring you to employ any police to protect us ; while this man, near by you, who has cost you any quantity of money, you have sympathy for him." —"Well," he says, "there are seven thousand such men in the city, and seven thousand more behind them." I suppose that amounts to so many votes. Said I, "Then it is the pressure that has been brought to bear upon you that has led you to grant it?" He flared up at that, and said he did not acknowledge any pressure. I told him there was no need for any liquor dealer to employ counsel ; the commissioners are the best counsel for them. They are bound to act in their favor ; they say that the leaning must be toward them, and not toward us. And that law which you read seems to be the simplest thing in the world. It appeared so then. And now the question is, what use is there of any law?

Mr. HERSEY. — The commissioners stated to this committee that all a party had to do was to state their objection, and a license could not be granted.

Mr. GOVE. — To a common victualler ; but an innholder has vested rights.

Mr. CROSBY. — Now, I could not understand on what grounds they could give a common victualler's license. If it was applied for under that first clause, it was rejected time and again. Do they have a full record of their business?

Mr. HART. — I do not think they do. They could not tell us what counsel appeared in a case.

Mr. CROSBY. — From all appearances they have a clerk there, who seemed to take down all this evidence. I hoped it was so, because we have not got through there yet. There is something further to do about this. I suppose, as I went through the case, listened to them and saw all their proceedings, this was the conclusion I came to : that they are anxious to keep in with all this class ; they want their votes, and they wish to keep on the right side of them.   They don't care so much whether this man gets his license, and think that, possibly, we can carry it still further.   It is within our power, you know, to bring it before one of the judges and have the license revoked, which takes it off their shoulders, while at the same time they have done all for this man that they could.

Mr. HERSEY. — You know they are appointed by the Mayor ; they are not elected.

Mr. FITZPATRICK. — You make a statement that the commissioners want the votes of these people.   To what do you have reference?

Mr. CROSBY. — Well, of course, their continuance in office depends on the votes of the people.

Mr. HERSEY. — Not hardly.

Mr. CROSBY. — It does in the last resort.

Mr. HERSEY. — We do not know what the Mayor will do.   It is outside of politics, as far as you can put it, to have them appointed by the Mayor.

Mr. CROSBY. — It was political reasons that ruled in this thing right straight through.   There was Mr. Whitmore ; he seemed to be one of the great moving powers in this thing.   At the first meeting he sat at the elbow of the chairman, and was in —

Mr. HERSEY. — What Whitmore was this?

Mr. FITZPATRICK. — Mr. Whitmore of the Council?

Mr. CROSBY. — Yes, sir.

Mr. FITZPATRICK. — Is it not in his ward?

Mr. CROSBY. — Yes, sir.

Mr. GOVE. — The reputation of the house is that of a common house of assignation — a resort for lewd and lascivious persons?

Mr. CROSBY. — That is what I am told.   The best way is to ask Capt. Adams, who was captain of the station in La Grange street for years.

Mr. FITZPATRICK. — Did he give it this reputation?

Mr. CROSBY. — I cannot say that he stated it quite as plainly as that, but that is the impression I got from him and from the officers at that station on La Grange street.   And, then, one of the sergeants there — I think Sergeant Thomas — gave his opinion in regard to it — that its reputation was not good, and that it was known to all the officers.   There were one or two officers there on Mr. Garvey's side who stated that they never heard anything against it.   This Sergeant Thomas was asked by Major Mahan if these officers who had been up around this house, day after day and night after night, should say there was nothing wrong, whether he should not think he was mistaken.   He said, " No ; if an officer of our station, who has been in the habit of going by there, says that he never saw anything wrong, I should think that he either would not see, or would not tell what he did see."   One of the officers there told me that they were sent for one Sunday by a woman who kept a boarding house on Warrenton street to take care of two young men, brothers.   One of them had drawn a knife on the other, and she was afraid he would kill him.   She said they had got their drink at the Briggs House. By the time the officers got there they had got this young man into bed, and they did not have to arrest him. While this was going on I was detained at my office two evenings quite late, and as I went out I saw, standing opposite the Briggs House, a young man and a young woman —

TESTIMONY OF SUPERINTENDENT OF POLICE ADAMS.

The CHAIRMAN. — Captain Adams, the committee have sent for you to have you give them what information you have in regard to the character of the Briggs House.

A. The Briggs House on Tremont street?

Q. Yes, sir.

A. Well, the Briggs House is about the same class of house that all these small innholders keep. There is nothing we can get to hold it, for evidence, to show that it is anything different from that. It is a place where girls on the street can go, and I have no doubt they do go, to meet men there ; the same as — well, perhaps, fifty others — not as many as that ; but, perhaps, say twenty.

Mr. HERSEY. — On what do you base the character of the house?

A. Well, they claim that they should have an innholder's license, because they have sleeping-rooms upstairs.

Q. But if they are not occupied?

A. Yes ; they claimed that it was. The commissioners hesitated. They have not got an innholder's license now. The commissioners would not grant it, because they were not innholders. They wanted it very much, and had several hearings ; but people objected very strongly at the Children's Mission to having it there. The commissioners had several hearings upon it, and finally refused to give them an innholder's license.

Q. Didn't the Children's Mission object to their giving them a common victualler's license?

A. I don't know but they did ; I should think very likely. I don't know their views.

Q. Could the commissioners grant a victualler's license if the adjoining estate objected? If the Children's Mission objected, could they legally grant them a license?

A. Well, I think the law is such that they can. It is applicable only to innholders, if you examine it.

Mr. CROSBY. — It is only applicable to common victuallers. And don't you recollect that Major Mahan made that point, that we could not object to an innholder's license, and that it was only a common victualler's license that we could object to?

Mr. HERSEY. — Mr. Gove knows about that.

Mr. GOVE. — The law applies to common victuallers, and not to innholders, who have vested rights.

Mr. ADAMS. — There was that point made by Major Mahan — that they did not abut.

Mr. CROSBY. — He tried to, but he had to withdraw that, because they had a gallery which united a building which is built up against our wall.

Capt. ADAMS. — Well, they were to take that away.

Mr. CROSBY. — He proposed to do that; but they did not. We took the ground that, if they did that it would require a new application; because an application for a license for the Briggs House, with that taken away, was not an application for a first-class license. But they did not take it away.

Mr. FITZPATRICK. — Whether or not, Capt. Adams, it is a house of ill-fame?

A. No; we could not make a case against it as a house of ill-fame. I am satisfied of that.

Mr. GOVE. — It is what we would call a house of assignation?

A. No, no; we could not do that.

Capt. ADAMS. — No, no; all these places where there are innholders' licenses have rooms. Of course, they could not get their licenses otherwise. They have to have some rooms where they can put up transient people.

Mr. FITZPATRICK. — Do you know whether they have sold liquor on Sunday since getting a license?

A. I do not think they have. Do you think they have, Mr. Crosby?

Mr. CROSBY. — Yes, I think so.

Mr. FITZPATRICK. — He says secretly, not publicly.

Mr. CROSBY. — I think the door is unfastened, so that any one can get in.

Capt. ADAMS. — I don't think the commissioners know that.

Mr. CROSBY. — I don't think they care to know anything about it. Their attention has been called to it. No formal complaint has been made, but they have been told of it. Don't you recollect when I called on you first and told you they had applied for an innholder's license, that you said, " He is not an innholder; it is nothing but a common drinking saloon?"

Capt. ADAMS. — Yes; and I say so now.

Mr. CROSBY. — Don't you remember Mr. Swan's being there?

Capt. ADAMS. — I do, very well.

Mr. CROSBY. — And what a strong statement he made in regard to the influence of such a place?

Capt. ADAMS. — Yes; and that was something peculiar — rather queer. When I was there Mr. Swan was very particular. And yet there is one right adjoining his yard; and they never could have got it there unless he had given his assent. That little back place there.

Mr. CROSBY. — Well, he explained that; I don't know how. He made some explanation about that being a very different sort of place from this. Still, I don't think he is right. Don't you recollect that you stated that no such place as that should be licensed in the vicinity of a school like the Winthrop, or in the vicinity of an institution like ours?

Capt. ADAMS. — I might have made that statement, although I might have stated it to you.

Mr. CROSBY. — No; this was before the commissioners. You spoke particularly of one case where you had seen four men drive up in a barouche and get out to get a drink.

Capt. ADAMS. — Certainly. There was no doubt, from the appearance of those men, who were in an open barouche, on Sunday — from the appearance of them any gentleman here would say that they drank. They got out and went in, and they were gone long enough. They would not go in there — all of them — for a cigar, and come out. We should say they drank something; but we cannot know. The appearances were to that effect.

Mr. CROSBY. — Now, is it not the business of the police officers, as they go by there, to report such things to the commissioners?

Capt. ADAMS. — No. Report it to their captains. Then the captains report it to me and I forward it.

Mr. GOVE. — They have special officers?

A. They have a special squad, who report direct; but that does not relieve us from enforcing the law.

Mr. CROSBY. — When you were there the reputation of the house was bad?

Capt. ADAMS. — Yes, sir; it is one of those houses — we have a good many of them in the city — they are not exactly notorious, but suspected of not being just right.

The CHAIRMAN. — If you had an officer who had travelled there three or four years, and you asked him, and he should say he did not see anything wrong, what should you think?

A. I should not think he told the truth. I should think he must know of the house.

Mr. CROSBY. — Were you there when Sergeant Thomas was on the stand?

Capt. ADAMS. — Yes, sir.

Mr. CROSBY. — Do you remember he said the very thing you state now? Mahan asked him — when you were not there — one or two policemen said they had been going by there for some time, and they had never seen anything out of the way, and they did not know but the reputation of the house was good — Sergeant Thomas was asked whether, in case these officers should say so, he would not think he was mistaken; and he said just what you have said: that he should think they did not see, or would not state what they did see. Now, haven't I stated his evidence there just as the Superintendent has stated it?

The CHAIRMAN. — I think so.

Mr. CROSBY. — I have stated to the committee what you have said.

Mr. HART. — Is that a place which, if you were a member of the commission, you would vote to license, knowing all the circumstances?

A. As I know them now, I think I should decline to license a place there next to that place. We have a good many places just as bad as that, or worse.

Mr. Crosby. — Suppose it was not an assignation house, would you license a place where the children of the Winthrop and primary schools must pass every day, and our children go in there, say two or three evenings a week and Sunndays? Would you license a drinking place there, anyway?

Capt. Adams. — Probably I should not be in favor of licensing so many of these places.

Mr. Crosby. — And you would choose your positions for them too, would you not?

Capt. Adams. — Yes, sir.

Mr. Hersey. — Well, I think we have got at the facts about this matter.

The Chairman. — That is all, Captain ; we are obliged to you for coming up.

Mr. Hart. — Is there anything more, Mr. Chairman, that you want of Mr. Crosby?

Mr. Chairman. — I do not think there is.

Mr. Hart. — I do not know that any question I can ask you would bring out anything.

Mr. Crosby. — I do not remember anything now, unless you want to ask me a question. The whole course of these commissioners is very singular, and it seems that they have great power over the law in allowing that man to go on selling without a license. There might, possibly, be an excuse up to the time in July when they refused him a license ; but from that time up to the 23d of September, when he had been refused positively, was it right for him to go on selling without a license?

The Chairman. — I presume they never make any trouble if a man makes application. They allow him to go on until his license is settled.

Mr. Crosby. — But it was refused. One thing I want to speak to you about. I am not there evenings after six o'clock, usually ; but just before going into the country I was obliged to work there late, until about half-past nine. As I left there, on the opposite sidewalk, I saw a young man and a woman standing up against the house ; a little further on, another man and two women ; and a little further on, a young girl ; and a little further on, others, I think about a dozen in all. As I was waiting for a car, I saw a girl come from Eliot street, alone, go into the Briggs House, and go back into one of these stalls. Then I saw this young man and woman, who were standing opposite, go over to the Briggs House. She went in and went back further — this was in warm weather, and the doors were open — and talked with the man in charge — I do not know his name, but the barkeeper — and this fellow stood looking in. He then left, went across, stayed a few minutes, and went back again ; went upstairs into the ladies' saloon ; came down in a moment and went into one of the stalls. Then I saw liquor carried in. While I stood there I saw that going on all the time ; and the next night I saw the same ; and that is what I am told by those about there is carried on all the time. If the question was whether, under that advertisement, they had the right to grant him anything in that class, it don't affect this case at all; it don't decide the question as to whether they had the right to grant a license that had been objected to.

Mr. HERSEY. — No, that is the point. They perhaps may not have asked the City Solicitor in reference to that particular question.

Mr. CROSBY. — I don't think it answers that question.

Mr. GOVE. — " Such notice shall set forth the name of the applicant in full and the character or class of license applied for." There are three or four different classes.

Mr. FITZPATRICK. — An innholder and a victualler are in the same class.

Mr. GOVE. —But with different prices.

Mr. FITZPATRICK. — There is an innholder's license, Class A, and a common victualler's license, Class A, each $400.

Mr. GOVE. — But the statutes do not recognize them.

Mr. CROSBY. — The commissioners have a paper printed, regulating the prices; that, I suppose, is a matter of convenience. One thing more, with reference to advertising. The law says that the advertising of these licenses is not sufficient which does not give persons notice of an opportunity to object. As it has been done, they are advertised only once; then objection must be made within ten days. Now, you can construe that law to read that it shall be advertised for ten days, and there certainly should be some alteration in that, to give more notice to the public.

Mr. HERSEY. — I think if the commissioners are right, it seems to me to be inexcusable for them to take advantage of the weakness of the statute, and give the benefit to the innholder, for the sake of shutting out an opportunity for the adjoining people to object.

Mr. GOVE. — Yes; for if they want to test the question, they can refuse, and have sombody bring a writ of mandamus to compel them.

Mr. HERSEY. — They could have sent up and given this institution an opportunity to put in their objection under the old application.

Mr. CROSBY. — Well, through the whole of this, everything has been done, it seems to me, to favor the other side. I think they possibly thought we might go farther, and bring it before one of the judges, as we shall.

TESTIMONY OF POLICE COMMISSIONER WALKER.

Mr. GOVE. — Col. Walker, we understood you to say when you were here the other day that when a party who owned an adjoining estate objected to the granting of a license, with the exception of innholders, who have vested rights, that stopped the issuing of the license?

A. Yes. The law does not permit us to issue a license if we understand that the owners of adjoining premises object to it within ten days. Then the law says that such license is null and void, and may be revoked by the court.

Mr. HERSEY. — Does the law compel you always to advertise?

A. The law compels us to advertise, and the advertisement is always made. About $5,000 worth of advertising has been done this year.

Mr. GOVE. — Supposing a party comes in and makes an application for an innholder's license, and the Board conclude that he ought not to have an innholder's license, but are willing to grant him a first-class victualler's license, would not that have to be advertised too?

A. As a rule, I should say yes ; and yet there might be a question, they both being first-class. The law says that the class shall be advertised, and, under that construction, — not, I say, as a rule ; as a rule we should probably do it, — but under that construction, they both being first-class, it would not be necessary.

Mr. HERSEY. — Supposing that under an application for an innholder's license you should want to grant a victualler's license, would not you then consider it incumbent on you to advertise ; because the adjoining estate could not object to one and could to the other, — so that you would be obliged, if you changed from what was first applied for — if you contemplated issuing a victualler's license instead of an innholder's — in order to give the adjoining estate an opportunity to object, you would then have to readvertise?

A. Well, that is a question which I think Mr. Gargan submitted to the City Solicitor. The law says, " Such notice shall set forth the name of the applicant in full, and the character or class of license applied for."

Q. Then, would not you consider that a person having objected on general grounds to the granting of an innholder's license, that that would be considered an objection to the granting of a common victualler's license?

A. No ; I can see where there might be a very great difference. The great thing that institutions and churches complain of is Sunday selling, and there is a great difference in the licenses in regard to that.

Q. Then, it would depend upon what the character of the objection was? Supposing it was not that they sold on Sunday, but that they sold at all, and that the place was improperly carried on week-days, you would heed that objection, would you not?

A. I should consider that objection, of course. Now, here is the point : " Licenses shall be of the following classes : *First class.* To sell liquors of any kind to be drunk on the premises." That takes in everybody. Then the law says : " Such notice shall set forth the name of the applicant in full, the class of the license applied for." The two laws are to be taken together, and the class will contain all the kinds which we divide it up into.

Q. You consider that *or* should be *and* in order to compel you to readvertise?

A. Yes ; I consider that character or class means about the same thing there. It means class. Taken in connection with the statute, it must mean leading class.

Mr. HART. — A party, appearing to make objection in one case, even if you should refuse an innholder's license, would not they be entitled to make the same objection to a victualler's license which they made to an innholder's?

A. That would depend altogether upon the evidence which came out in the first hearing on the innholder's license.

Mr. GOVE. — Supposing a party makes application for an innholder's license, and the party who owns the adjoining estate comes and objects, within the proper time, to the granting of a license there ; and thereupon, after hearing, the Board concludes that he ought not to have an innholder's license, the objecting party not withdrawing his objection, would you then grant a hearing to the party without notifying them?

A. As I say, that would depend much upon the circumstances. If, upon the first hearing on the innholder's license, we thought the case had been thoroughly investigated, and all the evidence put in, and then, when we came to consider the victualler's license, we considered, looking at the whole evidence, that they could not add any more evidence, why then we might not notify.

The CHAIRMAN. — If this gentleman objected to the selling of liquor in any form?

A. Simply that. I say each individual case would depend on circumstances. For instance, here is a party who objects to an innholder's license. They give us the whole evidence ; they might say they did not want liquor sold in any form, and on this ground we would notify them. Then, if we should see fit to consider the fact whether we will give them a lower grade of license, and, on looking it over, we should find that the evidence had already been given in a previous hearing, it would be unnecessary.

Q. Then, would you not consider that you would be debarred by the statute from granting a license?

A. That depends altogether upon a question of law and the circumstances. If the thing is illegal, we cannot grant it.

Mr. HERSEY. — I understood you to say that all that it was necessary for an adjoining estate to do was to give notice of their objection, and that you could not grant a license?

A. We could not grant a license under this statute.

Mr. GOVE. — Well, if a party made application for an innholder's license, and that was refused, and you were willing to grant him a first-class victualler's license, would he then have to make out a new application?

A. If the innholder's license was refused?

Q. Yes.

A. Our practice has been, sometimes, to make a new application, and sometimes not. I think, in some cases, we have done both. We have to treat every case upon the circumstances and the facts developed. Of course the law is the guide ; but the circumstances or facts developed, either in the hearing or by the officers outside, decide what action we shall take, each case differing in details.

Mr. HERSEY. — Would you consider that, having acted upon

an application for an innholder's license, and a week or two having elapsed, would you consider that a case still pending in which you could take action upon granting another kind of a license?

A. If a party came to us and said, "You refused me an innholder's license; now I am willing to take a less objectionable one," we should consider it perfectly right to take it up again.

Mr. HERSEY. — I don't see why. It changes entirely the character of what is to be done. It might open up an entirely new set of objections.

Col. WALKER. — With one single exception, there is no objection to an innholder's license that there would not be to a victualler's; and that is, the selling from twelve o'clock Saturday night to twelve o'clock Sunday night.

Mr. GOVE. — But the party objecting would have great power in regard to a person who was going to sell under a victualler's license more than he would over a person who was to sell as an innholder, because, as you said the other day, an innholder has vested rights. The party who owns the adjoining estate may object to a victualler, while with an innholder the statute is not effective.

Mr. HERSEY. — So that he might not put his objection in writing, in order to compel the law to take effect, not knowing that it was contemplated to grant a victualler's license. I might object for an adjoining estate, and say: This man has applied for an innholder's license, and I don't want him to have it; but if I understood he had applied for a victualler's license, my objection would be effective, and I would put in evidence.

Mr. HART. — Supposing a man should ask for a license for a house adjoining mine, and I should go in and object — should not give you any reason, but should object to that man's having a license — could he get a license?

A. There are licenses of a certain kind that he could not get.

Q. Could he get a license?

A. No. [*Reads*]: "If before the expiration of the ten days following the publication of the notice, as required by the preceding section, the owner of any real estate adjoining the premises described in an application for a license to be exercised by a common victualler to sell liquors to be drunk on the premises, notifies the licensing board in writing that he objects to the granting of the license, no license to sell intoxicating liquors to be drunk on said premises shall be granted."

Q. Plain, is it not?

A. Plain.

Q. Now, in the case of the Briggs House: they applied for a license, and the Children's Mission people objected. An innholder's license was refused. Afterwards, they were granted a victualler's license. Did you have any rights to grant them a victualler's license?

A. I will say we should not have granted it unless we had the right.

Q. Are you familiar with that case, and with what has been done there?

A. I am familiar with all but one or two hearings.

The CHAIRMAN. — You have records kept?

A. Yes, sir.

Q. What is your general opinion of the character of the Briggs House?

A. My general opinion of the character of the Briggs House is, that the statements made with regard to it — made by certain parties — were a great deal exaggerated.

Mr. HART. — It don't seem to me we care anything about what the character of the house is. It may be the best house in Boston. Here is simply an adjoining owner objecting. No matter whether it is good, bad, or indifferent. It may be the Parker House.

The CHAIRMAN. — He says every case rests on its merits.

Col. WALKER. — No ; I said every case inside the law.

Mr. HART. — In my own house he distinctly says that — I objecting — that man cannot have the license. Now, here is the Briggs House ; the Children's Mission objects, and he has got a license. I want to understand it.

Major JONES. — Pardon me if I make a suggestion. The first question to be determined is whether you are an abuttor. There is a plan which was submitted by the petitioners, which they claim is correct. Here is Tremont street ; here is the Briggs House, running back and forming an L here ; there is a passage-way that runs down to that point ; there is a bridge running across there ; here is the Chinese laundry, which runs down to somewhere here ; this part here, that wide part there, is what has heretofore been used when this had a hotel license as a part of the lodging-rooms, where no liquor was sold.

The CHAIRMAN. — Without lodging-rooms they could not get a license as an innholder?

Major JONES. — Yes ; they had some there.

The CHAIRMAN. — They had a hotel register too, didn't they?

Major JONES. — Yes, sir ; all made up within about half an hour.

The CHAIRMAN. — And they had another down at the bindery?

Major JONES. — Yes, another at a bookbinder's who had been dead thirteen years, I think. Now, the answer to the suggestion, that the Mission had the right to object because they were abuttors, was met by the display of this plan. In the first place, they say, there is the Chinese laundry that separates the Briggs House from the Mission. In the next place there is a passage-way, and all the possible connection the Briggs House could have there was because they put a bridge across that passage-way to connect these sleeping-rooms with the Briggs House. Upon a conference, a majority of the commission were satisfied, and I understand from Mr. Gargan that the question was submitted to the City Solicitor.

Col. WALKER. — He went himself.

Major JONES. — It did not appear that they had a legal right to claim that they were abuttors, and hence their objection to granting a common victualler's license was of no consequence, although we examined this upon the ground whether this was a nuisance, or whether it was so annoying to these people that it should not be granted. But upon the display of that plan, which did not appear to be objected to, it appeared that they were not legally abuttors. It appears that after the application was made for the Briggs House to be licensed as a hotel that lease was discontinued, or the evidence was that that lease was discontinued, and that the passage-way leading from here to there was thoroughly, substantially, and permanently closed up ; so there was no access from the Briggs House to these sleeping-rooms.

Mr. HERSEY. — That was done to evade the statute ?

Major JONES. — Undoubtedly ; but it has a legal effect.

Mr. HERSEY. — Do you know, as a matter of fact, that this part is not now occupied by this party as a lodging-room ?

Major JONES. — Well, I have not examined it personally, but the sworn testimony was that the entrance to the Briggs House, which was formerly there, had been firmly and permanently closed up.

Mr. HERSEY. — In what way ; by its being locked ?

Major JONES. — By its being fastened. We should not consider it closed if it was only locked.

Mr. HERSEY. — Why might not any party evade the law in the same way by running a partition down around his own estate and letting it to another party ?

Major JONES. — Well, sir, the whole business is an evasion of the law — the whole liquor traffic.

Mr. HART. — The commissioners themselves are not trying to evade the law.

Major JONES. — I hope not. But when you submit to us a proposition and ask us to pass upon it —

Col. WALKER. — Where parties stand on strict technical law, we are bound to stand on it. If a man come to me and says, " I have cut off and sold ten inches of my estate to Tom Smith," we cannot say that that does not kill the whole effect of the law about adjoining estates.

Mr. HERSEY. — Would you grant a license to a party who thus evaded the law ?

A. That would depend entirely on circumstances.

Mr. GOVE. — I suppose if it was the only objection ; of the man keeping the place, the manner of his conducting his business was proper under the law, and, as far as the Board knew, or had any evidence, he did it carefully and well, and kept a decent, respectable place, and made that sale so that his estate would not join, and the estate was satisfied that it was solely for that purpose, as a matter of law that would be a fraud, of course.

A. It would be an evasion of the law ; I do not think there would be any fraud about it. I suppose there would not be any fraud if a man sold me a piece of five or ten inches of an estate. It would be done to evade the law, but it would not necessarily be a fraud in the eyes of the law.

Q. Not as regards creditors ; but would not it be in regard to this form of law ?

A. It would be an evasion of the law.

Q. In other words, putting the property out of his hands so that it would effect the legal position of the rest of his property?

A. A *bona fide* sale of a piece of property to effect the rest of his property, would not be a fraud. My position is this : that a *bona fide* sale of a piece of property for the purpose of affecting the rest of his property, would not be a fraud in the legal definition of a fraud.

Q. But, supposing that the Board was satisfied that this transaction, that is to say, the selling or deeding a certain strip of property, was done solely for the purpose of evading the law, and you were not satisfied that it was a *bona fide* sale, what would be your construction then?

A. If I was not satisfied that it was a *bona fide* sale I would most decidedly take it as no sale at all.

Q. Well, then, to carry out the inquiry : would you believe that a man would make a deed to another party of a strip of his property, six, eight, or ten feet wide — I mean to a man who had no interest in the adjoining estate — who could not put anything upon it, — would you be likely to believe that that was a *bona fide* sale?

A. It would depend altogether on the evidence that was brought. I cannot give you an abstract opinion on anything of that kind.

Q. Well, I offer that as a proposition. Suppose here is a party who owns an estate, say twenty feet wide ; another party owns another estate right up adjoining his ; this party owning this estate wants a liquor license, and this adjoining party objects ; he turns around and makes a conveyance of a strip of his property, six, eight, or ten feet wide, and then comes in and says that this party is not an adjoining owner.

A. I can conceive of cases where he might make a *bona fide* sale. If it was for the benefit of his property, he would do it.

Q. Well, would anybody be foolish enough to purchase it?

A. The whole question depends on circumstances.

Mr. FOLAN. — If that man should partition off his property, wouldn't he evade the law technicality of the statute, just as a man would who made an assignment of his wages?

A. Well, we will let every man settle that for himself.

Mr. GOVE. — Well, we usually break those assignments when we try them in court.

Major JONES. — The magistrates do not regard them very highly.

Col. Walker. — I have several clients I will have to send to you.

Mr. GOVE. — You will find you can get your spear under them somehow. Now, take this matter of the Briggs House. I suppose that your facts are to date at the time of the date of the petition?

A. The gaining of the facts.

Q. Now, suppose a man makes an application on the first of May for the granting of a license. At that time his estate is so situated that, under the law, he could not have a license. The matter goes along from that time up to some time in September, and the only change that is made in the situation of affairs is the releasing by him of a part of his estate, so as to avoid adjoining owner's rights.   Would that fact have any bearing upon the granting of his license?

A.   Yes ; I think it would come under pretty nearly the same head as one case I know of where an adjoining owner objected, and afterwards withdrew his objection.   We took up the old application and granted it.

Q.   Well, suppose this party did not withdraw?

A.   Well, I say, the legal objection having been gotten rid of, it might stand in the same way as if the man had withdrawn his objection.

Q.   Well, was that the ground that the Board took in granting a first-class victualler's license to the Briggs House ; his having had this part of the estate struck out of his lease?

A.   I cannot tell what the specific grounds were ; a good many of the details have escaped my memory.   I have no doubt that was one of the grounds ; that is, that took away the legal objection of having an adjoining estate there.   The details of the grounds I do not remember, any more than I do those of 500 other cases.   I can simply tell you the facts as they exist.

Q.   Do all the grounds of objection in the various cases appear on record at the office?

A.   Oh, no.   Some one will object on some ground, and we will give him a show and let him go on and say all sorts of things.   He will object on the ground of its being a disorderly ground, and we will let him go on.

Q.   I refer particularly to cases before the commissioners.   Do the grounds on which they object appear on record in the proceedings?

A.   I should say they generally did.   There is a good deal of evidence there in all of these cases which is not evidence ; just like a thousand things with regard to police business.   We know things that we cannot prove by evidence, like thousands of things you are morally certain of but cannot prove in court.

Q.   I should like to find out why this license should be granted and the license asked for by Mr. Fallon, on Dudley street, was refused?

A.   That is more than I can tell.   I do not remember the facts in Fallon's case at all.

Q.   His case was very similar to this.   He owned two estates, and he made a conveyance of one of the estates, that adjoining the church.   The church objected to his being licensed.   He made a conveyance of one estate, and his license was still refused.

A.   I do not remember particularly why it was refused any more than that there was a church there.   That was one reason ; but as to all the details, it is actually impossible for me to remember.

Q.   You could not be expected to do so in the matter of two thousand cases.   But here is also the same as a church, because the institution is carried on for beneficiary purposes — for parties unable to provide for themselves.   Here is the Children's Mission right here, and immediately back of this estate, if I remember correctly, is the Young Women's Christian Association.

Major Jones. — That is on Warrenton street.

Mr. Gove. — Yes, but its back is on the street immediately back of it, is it not?

Major Jones. — Warrenton street is in the rear. I don't know whether there is a connection there or not.

Mr. Gove. — Now, then, take a case right here, near the Young Women's Christian Association rooms. Some weeks ago I remember calling attention to it — I think it was to you, Major — in regard to this estate at the corner of Tremont and Warrenton streets.

Major Jones. — No, not to me.

Mr. Gove. — To Mr. Gargan. I understand the ground for refusal was that it was so near?

Major Jones. — Not wholly.

Mr. Gove. — That was opposed, I understand, on this ground ; and if it applied there, why should it not apply here, where there are two or three estates in question.

Col. Walker. — For the very reason that the circumstances might be entirely different. The general reason might be put on record, and the circumstances might show an entirely different state of affairs.

Mr. Gove. — Could there be a more notorious set of circumstances applied to any case than where the officers testified that the place has a bad reputation, not particularly for a house of ill-fame, but that it has associations connected with it, and surrounding it, that show that it is a resort for prostitutes, and a house of assignation ; and where the people near to it are carrying on an establishment for the improvement of the morals, and the education of children whose parents are unable, by reason of their misfortune or vicious circumstances, to give them proper education ; where there is a public school within three hundred feet of the same place, and another a very short distance from there ; where boys and girls are passing daily, — do you think, taking all these circumstances into consideration, it could be more injurious?

A. If you ask me a general question, without applying it to any particular house, I should say no. If you refer to any particular house, I should want to see the facts upon which that allegation was made in regard to that particular case.

Q. Now, we will apply it to this one particular case, the case of the Briggs House. It has been stated here by Mr. Crosby, who is connected with the Children's Mission, that there was evidence introduced before the Board by himself, by the master of the Winthrop School, by Superintendent Adams, by Sergeant Thomas of Station 4, and by various people who were somewhat familiar with the circumstances about this establishment, that a bad class of people were constantly going there ; that it had for years substantially had the reputation of being a place resorted to by that class of people that I have suggested, and that the facts were stated before the Board at the hearing. Now, this Children's Mission, being where it is, the Winthrop School where it is, the

Primary school where it is, and the people who attend it passing by this establishment constantly during the day, would not that of itself show that it was hardly the place to grant a license?

A. Well, the only way I can answer that is, that the commission, after looking upon all the evidence — not upon general statements, as you have given — and the character of the house for two or three years, did not think, from the evidence offered, it was.

Q. I suppose the commissioners themselves, personally, knew nothing about the place?

A. I remember when I first went into the Board we cut down their license for two years. They had had an innholder's license for two years. They could not get an innholder's license when Col. Russell and I were there until they got an innholder's license under the law. Aldermen Stebbins, Guild, and Faunce gave them their innholder's license, and we gave them their innholder's. So there were two Boards who investigated them. Curtis Guild appeared there for them.

Major Jones. — Curtis Guild appears now for them.

The Chairman. — When was this license given?

Major Jones. — In 1879.

The Chairman. — What time?

Major Jones. — In May.

The Chairman. — I didn't know but it was just before election.

Col. Walker. — They took it away from the commission and put it into the Board of Aldermen, because they supposed we would cut it down. I think all the committee recommended it. They signed it, and no questions were asked.

Mr. Hersey. — They signed it in the way we sign any document, recommending the secretary to pay the debt of the United States in currency.

Col. Walker. — Under the law as it then stood the Board of Aldermen thought it was a proper place to grant an innholder's license, and I think they must have known at that time — the committee must have known — that they were innholders the year before, and were applying for a victualler's. Then we examined into it, and gave them an innholder's.

Mr. Hersey. — Do you know as a matter of fact that he has stopped selling on Sunday, because we have testimony that they are selling?

A. That may be; but, then, there is something gained by it. We do not deny that liquor is sold on Sunday where it ought not to be. I would not, as a matter of fact, say that it was so; but I say the law says it shall not be sold, and if the doors are closed, it is so much gained.

Q. Well, if so many go in, there would not be much gained?

A. The men who frequent the place will go there; a man who was transient would not go in to take a drink. So that, on the general ground, there is a great deal gained when you get that step, — when you get the doors closed and the shutters up.

Mr. Gove. — Do you remember of Sergeant Thomas, of Station 4, appearing before the Board?

A. I remember he was there, but I do not remember his testimony.

Q. It has been stated here to us, I think by both Mr. Crosby and Superintendent Adams, that he testified as regards this place; that it was a place resorted to by a bad class of people, and was not a place of good reputation.

A. Well, there would come in another question which only shows how this develops and ramifies all around. What do you mean by being resorted to by bad people?

Q. A house of assignation.

A. Well, we never had any evidence that they made it a house of assignation. There are some of the quietest places in Boston resorted to by prostitutes and thieves. In that locality there are undoubtedly a great many women who are kept or who keep themselves and who are barred out from social position. Now, these people have got to eat and drink. A murderer has got to eat and he has got to drink. He will go there, as I know of one or two cases, but nothing improper takes place. They sit and talk. They cannot go into decent society. They cannot come to Parker's. They have got to go somewhere to eat. So a place may be reported to be a resort for prostitutes and thieves, and yet be conducted in a perfectly proper manner, and should have a license, without doubt. It is only where a place is the resort of prostitutes openly for assignation,— as the Stanley House was three years ago, where we sent officers in and found the men in the reception room putting their hands under the women's dresses, right in the open reception room, and we broke it up, — or where there is criminal connection that you can prove or have good grounds for, that you can take exception to. He will go to a place resorted to by prostitutes for a perfectly innocent purpose — for food and drink. That place will get the reputation of being a bad place. I have known places where they had the hardest reputation, but after all I found out that the place was perfectly innocent as far as that was concerned. These people went there, and, therefore, it was said they went there for assignation and improper purposes. It is no good reason.

Mr. HART. — How many people do you think you have had come into the commissioners' office to say a good word for Mr. Garvey?

A. A great many.

Q. Hundreds?

A. I could not say ; but we had a good many. There is another element. We had some sympathy for Mr. Garvey on another account. Here was a man wounded at Fredericksburg and at Gettysburg, and incapacitated for work. He was a soldier all through the war. He had his money all in there. Now, there is an element that comes in there. If that place can be properly conducted without being a nuisance to its neighbors, that is another question. There was a great deal of sympathy expressed for him by a great many people.

Mr. GOVE. — Here is another question, then. At the first hearing Major Mahan appeared, according to the testimony, and at the next hearing it took two counsel.

A. I do not remember now, but that would not be anything surprising.

Q. Well, supposing in the community a story goes abroad that with one man for counsel a license is refused, and as, in this case, twice refused, according to the statement made by Mr. Crosby, the same counsel appearing at the first two hearings, and then at the last hearing another counsel came in, who has the reputation of being wonderfully successful in taking out licenses — whether or not there is not some ground for complaint upon the part of these abuttors?

A. Well, if you mean to insinuate, Mr. Gove, that any one counsel at this bar has been remarkably successful in getting licenses, because he is such counsel, I absolutely and utterly deny it.

Q. I do not do it, because I do not know it.

A. The insinuation is pretty broad. I do not care what the public impression is, I utterly and absolutely deny any such insinuation for myself, personally, from beginning to end. Now, I will answer your question. There is no particular reason why it should be restricted to one counsel any more than in court. If you are counsel in a case, and if somebody else came up and wanted an opportunity to be heard, we should not object. If Mr. Crosby had wanted to get Mr. Sidney Bartlett, or Mr. Morse, or Mr. Hutchins, we should let them come in. If, after he had had one hearing, he wanted to let some other counsel come in, we should not object. So it is nothing strange that additional counsel did appear in any case before us.

Mr. HART. Well, the matter of sympathy for a man in any circumstances — would you let that govern you?

A. It would naturally be an element, as in all cases. I suppose there is not one of us who can try a case — I do not suppose a jury can try a case — in law but what there would be a certain bias or tendency, one way or the other, if such facts appeared.

TESTIMONY OF POLICE COMMISSIONER JONES.

Mr. HART. — Major Jones, did you ever tell Mr. Crosby that you had refused to grant this man a license?

A. Yes, sir.

Q. When you told him that did you believe you should ever grant him a license of any kind?

A. No, sir.

Q. Did you believe it was a good thing and a right thing for the commissioners to do, to grant this license, under all the circumstances?

A. Well, sir, I ought not to be inquired of in regard to my personal feelings. Perhaps my personal wishes and ideas might not in all things be those of the commissioners. When I sit with the commission I submit to the majority rule, and I claim that I have no right to introduce there my personal judgment. As a general thing we are harmonious, and if I have an idea that conflicts, I do not think I ought to speak of it outside. I think we sit there as the ministers of the law, and we have no right to do anything except to say what is our duty under the law. I am a prohibitionist in sentiment and practice, but I sit there as a commissioner to administer the law of the land, whatever it may be.

Q. That is true and that is right. Supposing you sat there, and a license was to be granted to a party, and in your best judgment of the subject, down in the bottom of your heart, this man ought not to have any license, what should you do?

A. I should submit to the majority, sir. That is what I do, and claim that I have no right except to fairly treat the judgment of the majority, although it might be different from mine.

Mr. HERSEY. — You do not always have unanimous action?

A. You do not in the Board of Aldermen.

Q. I did not know but you might, in granting licenses. But there is never one granted unless two vote for it?

A. No, sir. I think, Mr. Chairman, you want to get at a better history of this case than you have. Because, whatever my individual ideas may be, you want to know the history of the case, if you are going to pass upon the question whether the commission have acted wisely and properly. It is evident from the line of inquiry that you have not got all the facts.

Mr. HERSEY. — I suppose we would like to have them, and we would like to have the commissioners give them to us.

Major JONES. — Well, sir, whatever my individual judgment might be about the Briggs House, is not of any consequence at all, of course. This gentleman applied for a license as an innholder, and made a very strenuous effort for it. And upon the evidence, the Board felt that he was not entitled to it. Even if Mr. Crosby had not presented any objection, this man would not have had a license as an innholder. He had kept his place open later than he ought to have done, although, under the law, he had the right to keep it open all night; and he kept it open on Sunday, and sold liquor, and he had the right to do that. But he enjoyed his rights to the fullest extent. During the year I called his attention to it, that he was not giving satisfaction, but he thought he had the right to do as he liked. When the time came for him to apply, I gave the commission the benefit of my knowledge. I think if Mr. Crosby had not been before us, the commission would have been unanimous in refusing; for we said to Mr. Garvey and his friends, you shall not have the sanction or protection of any license which will protect you further in selling liquor on Sunday and at night in the way you are conducting your business. And before any hearing was had, we had come to that conclusion. The advertisement of Mr. Garvey occurred in May. His application for a license was May 27th. but immediately we had arrived substantially at that conclusion, although by no formal action. On the 6th of June — a long time after the ten days expired when Mr. Crosby by right could file his objection — Mr. Crosby filed his objection;

but Mr. Garvey had then been brought down to the limits and been notified.

Mr. Hart. — What was the date of the advertisement?

Major Jones. — The 27th of May.

Mr. Hart. — The objection was filed on the 6th of June. Didn't that let him in?

Major Jones. — It did. But before Mr. Crosby made any objection the Board had considered it, and our judgment was made up substantially that it should not be granted. And then, when the objection was made, that, of course, was simply an addition to the strength of the judgment of the commission. Then the proposition was made that these parties had no right to object to his having a license as a victualler, because they were not abuttors; and this petition of Mr. Garvey's was brought in — the petition for a hearing. We had, substantially, notified Mr. Garvey that he could not have a license, although there had been no record made of it. This petition came in on the 26th of July. It is addressed to the Board, and reads as follows: —

The undersigned would respectfully represent that he would desire to be heard by counsel upon the question as to whether or not he shall be granted an innholder's license, and a license of the *first-class*, to sell intoxicating liquors upon the premises No. 271 Tremont street, in the city of Boston, being the main portion of the premises described in his applications for said licenses, now upon file; and your petitioner now withdraws his request to use any portion of the premises numbered two hundred and seventy-three (273) Tremont street for the purposes abovenamed. Your petitioner would respectfully state that the grounds upon which he prays to be heard are as follows: —

First. — Because he avers that the law is unchanged, so far as granting an innholder's license, and a license to sell intoxicating liquors of the *first-class, to be an innholder,* by chapter 255 of the Acts, A.D. 1881, or by any other statute of this Commonwealth. Therefore, your petitioner alleges it would be a great injustice to him to draw the inference that the Legislature intended to include the innholder, especially as the journal of that body (and he desires to introduce this fact) shows that an amendment was *offered* and *rejected* to include innholders among those where such objection as is provided in said statute by the owner of an adjoining estate must be final and conclusive as to the granting of such a license, thereby indicating conclusively, as your petitioner claims, that the intent and purpose of the Legislature was to *exempt* the innholder from the operation of the law that applies to common victuallers.

Second. — Your petitioner avers that the remonstrants against granting him an innholder's license did not seasonably file the objection to said license, and have not, in a legal or formal manner, complied with the provisions of the law relating thereto: and, further, your petitioner avers that *they are not the owners of the adjoining estate;* and he respectfully refers to a copy of the lease annexed, containing a description of the premises he occupies, and for which he desires to be licensed to carry on his business aforesaid, to wit, in the building No. 271 Tremont street. He also refers to the plan of the three estates, viz., 271, 273 Tremont street, and the Children's Mission (so-called), by which it will be seen that the building occupied by the Children's Mission is not the adjoining estate to No. 271 Tremont street.

This plan, which he presents with this petition, was made by the proper authorities at City Hall, where the original may be found in the Sewer Department. The above reasons and others your petitioner prays to present, that his rights, under the law regulating the sale of intoxicating liquors and governing an innholder, may be determined, to the end that he may not be damaged in his business and put to great loss, for the sole reason that the remonstrants object to the right given you by the law to license him to carry on said business, under due restrictions and regulations.

W. H. Whitmore, Esq., of the Common Council, desires to be notified when the hearing is assigned.

Respectfully,

PETER A. GARVEY,
271 Tremont street.

Upon that hearing Mr. Curtis Guild came in and recommended that this license should be granted; and Mr. Whitmore, of the Common Council, appeared and was exceedingly earnest in his express wish that it should be granted. Mr. Howard, of the Howard Watch Company, on Tremont street, and Mr. Morey, of the Manufacturing Company. All these gentlemen came and said they had been to this establishment at all hours, and they had found nothing there but what might be found in any ordinary restaurant. And they thought, under the circumstances, we were doing this man a great wrong not to give him a license as an innholder. But, certainly, it was suggested, we could not refuse him a license as a victualler. Mr. Crosby also appeared. There was some evidence contradictory. There was some evidence that the place was resorted to by girls on the street, but no more so than in restaurants of that class. It is a universal fact, known to everybody who has any sort of knowledge, that all these girls go to every inn, not excluding the Parker House or any of these fashionable or unobjectionaole places. But the evidence was contradictory. Some said it was quite as good a place as any house of this kind. Among these gentlemen were Mr. Curtis Guild and Mr. Howard. They filled our room two or three days, and showed that this man ought to have a license.

Mr. HART. — This is a very interesting document. [Reads.]

This indenture, made the twelfth day of July, in the year of our Lord one thousand eight hundred and seventy-seven, between Charles W. Galloupe of Boston, in the County of Suffolk and Commonwealth of Massachusetts, of the first part, and Peter A. Garvey, of Boston, in the County of Suffolk and Commonwealth aforesaid, of the second part,

Witnesseth, That the said party of the first part, in consideration of the rent and covenants hereinafter reserved and contained, and on the part of the party of the second part and his representatives to be said, observed, kept, and performed, doth by these presents lease, demise, and let unto the said party of the second part the wooden building situated on the westerly side of, and numbered two hundred and seventy-one (271) on, Tremont street in said Boston, said building containing a store and two tenements, with woodshed in rear.

The gas fixtures of the entire building are the property of the lessor.

Signed, sealed, and delivered in presence of

A. T. WHITING.

C. W. GALLOUPE. [Seal]
P. A. GARVEY. [Seal]

Now, in the name of heaven, are there any two men, Police Commissioners or not, who would accept that as evidence?

Col. WALKER. — I am not prepared to say how far it went as evidence. It was filed with the papers.

Mr. HART. — The whole process is scratched out. It is not a lease in any sense of the word.

Col. WALKER. — This has been filed with us as being a copy of a paper.

Mr. HART. — If it had been a counterfeit bill you would have filed it?

Col. WALKER. — Certainly. We do not propose to cover up anything. That is just the reason why we put such papers on file.

Mr. HERSEY. — This is the key?

Col. WALKER. — It is a paper put on file.

Mr. HERSEY. — It is the only thing that can determine whether it was a leasing of the premises or not?

Col. WALKER. — Not by any means. A bogus lease might be put on file.

Mr. HERSEY. — This is the evidence you had that the property had changed?

Major JONES. — No, sir.

Mr. HERSEY. — Can there be any other?

Col. WALKER. — Suppose a bogus lease was put in, there might be other evidence entirely. I do not pretend to say in this case, because I do not remember. But, when a statement is made as to the strength of that lease, I say I do not know how far that evidence was used, or whether any attention was paid to the lease as a paper.

Mr. GOVE. — Well, here is a written paper, undoubtedly drawn by some counsel, representing or purporting to be a copy of a written statement which a man has, which gives him certain rights in a certain estate. But here are the conditions entirely stricken out; nothing there but a simple description of the property and a description of the parties, the day of the granting of the lease, the signatures of the two parties and the subscribing witness. Well, now, then, it looks a little peculiar, at least, that a party should furnish such a piece of paper as that to your Board for you to act upon and consider in connection with this case, because it is entirely outside of any of the ordinary proceedings.

Col. WALKER. — And it may be that we so viewed it.

Major JONES. — It is a common exhibition of the stupidity of counsel, rather than anything else.

Mr. HERSEY. — Would you not have to have some evidence that this had changed hands, — that this did not join the Children's Mission?

Major JONES. — Yes. I have no doubt there was a great deal of parole evidence.

Mr. HERSEY. — It must be something in writing? A verbal lease you would not consider?

Col. WALKER. — Why not? When half of the estates in Boston are on verbal leases?

Mr. HERSEY. — It seems to me that would not authorize the commissioners to issue a license.

Col. WALKER. — Let us take a case. I suppose you have had an interest in real estate held under a verbal lease?

Mr. HERSEY. — Yes, sir.

Col. Walker. — How are you going to prove it?

Mr. Hersey. — I should suppose you were to prove it.

Col. Walker. — Well, you come before me and want to prove that you have leased certain premises. How are you going to prove it except on the testimony of yourself and the other party.

Mr. Hersey. — Now, was there, as a matter of fact, any other evidence than that?

Col. Walker. — I do not know that there was any other. I have no doubt that the commission acted in good faith as far as that is concerned. I know there was evidence and conversation outside of any paper. There was a very long discussion and these maps were there. The whole matter was very lengthily discussed.

The Chairman. — Is not that lease stronger than anything else you could get? Was it not the best evidence you could have?

Col. Walker. — In some respects it was. It would be likely to control; but, say an imperfect document came to you, not fully made out. Mr. Gove knows that if a paper goes into court, the rule is that you cannot go behind a written instrument. Yet there are a thousand instruments which are made imperfectly and evidence is brought to control them. Take the case of Mr. Hersey letting property on a verbal lease; that is an imperfect lease. This is an imperfect lease; but we considered that we ought to admit his evidence and let it go for what it is worth.

Mr. Fitzpatrick. — It is a question of granting a license after an innholder's has been refused.

Mr. Hart. — I interrupted Major Jones in his statement.

Major Jones. — It may seem very funny that I should take up this part of my story by saying that this was not a mere objection to the lease. The lease was brought in with the petition. I do not think we paid any attention to it. I don't think I ever heard it read until now. It was filed with the papers. I regarded it as simply a piece of paper; it was not testimony; we relied upon sworn testimony. One point was, that that piece of estate which was connected with the Briggs House by a bridge never was proved to have contained a drop of intoxicating liquor, or that there was any intention on the part of Mr. Garvey to sell anything there. It was simply used for lodging-rooms. And when that was suggested, that notwithstanding they were only lodging-rooms, yet they were a part of the estate, then the suggestion was offered that they could be only technically so, because connected by a bridge, and the proposition was made in good faith to discontinue that connection over the bridge. We did not pay any attention to any of these documents, they are so easily gotten up; in many instances they are simply gotten up for a blind, to throw dust in our eyes; but we found parties who knew something about it, and took their testimony; and that is the testimony we acted upon. There was no evidence that we could extort from any one that they had ever been used for any other purpose than as sleeping-rooms.

Mr. Hersey. — Right here — was there any evidence that these front rooms were used for any other purpose?

A. Oh, yes, sir; there was. On this upper floor there is what they call a restaurant or ladies' saloon, and in the rear there are little rooms in which there are tables for what they call parties, and over these are sleeping-rooms. The only evidence was that liquor was sold in the parlor, in the ladies' room, and in the rooms for private parties. There was none ever carried over the bridge at all. So we do not care a picayune about their papers. They never amount to shucks. We know what the drift of things is, and know what counsel are driving at. We prefer to hear the testimony of the individual, and submit him to such investigation as will test the truth of what he says. Although there was an offer made to show that the passage-way was not as wide as it was shown to be, and an offer also to show that the laundry was the property of the owner of the Briggs House, yet there was never any offer to show that the laundry and the passage-way were in any way occupied by or connected with the Briggs House, except by a bridge.

The CHAIRMAN. — They had the right of way?

A. Of course, but it runs between the laundry and the Briggs House, not between the laundry and the Children's Mission. I have always had a great deal of tender sympathy for the Children's Mission and places like this; but I have not any right to claim that my colleagues have not just as much care for them as I, and, in general, we agree. Mr. Whitmore and other gentlemen in the City Government came to us and gave us assurances in such a positive way that we could not say we do not believe you; you come here with a lie in your mouth, or with some other motive than to give us the facts. We told them what the objections were, and asked them to relieve us. We said, " You cannot ask this if these objections exist," and they said they did not exist. One gentleman on the opposite side of the street complained that he was disturbed. He usually sat up until twelve o'clock, and he had no objection except that he did not want to be disturbed after twelve o'clock. If an innholder's license had been granted, he could still have complained of the place as a nuisance, if it was a nuisance; the granting of a victualler's license would cut off that right; but so far as the police reports come to us, this license has been very carefully observed. I take that place upon my beat, and give it a very careful scrutiny; and it appears to me, late at night, that this man has kept fairly within the limits of his license. I have watched him, not for any vindictive purpose, but simply to test the sincerity of the man and his friends, as to whether he would carefully observe his license.

Mr. HERSEY. — Have you any record of the testimony in this case?

A. Yes, sir; substantially.

Col. WALKER. — The testimony is taken by the clerk of course; not in shorthand. We instruct him to give a general idea of what is testified to.

Q. Whether there was a conflict of testimony between your officers; — Sergeant Thomas and Capt. Adams testified, as I understand, against the character of the place?

A. Yes, sir. But you will bear in mind that Capt. Adams' testimony related to a period before 1878, when he was captain of

Station 4. He has for three or four years been Superintendent of Police, and therefore has no personal knowledge.

Q. Does the same party carry on the business now as then?

A. Yes, sir. Thomas, up to last January, was what was called night officer, and he did not have any knowledge of what had been done before midnight. He is day sergeant now.

Col. WALKER. — When Col. Russell was in the Board there was a place below there, kept by a man named Kendall, that was complained of twice, and we broke the license. We never had any complaint against Garvey's place.

Q. The Children's Mission complained, didn't they?

A. They did not complain then. There was no complaint last year. You understand that a man who has an innholder's license may keep open seven days in the week and twenty-four hours in the day, and every man may drink himself drunk on the premises; but a victualler is restricted from six o'clock in the morning until twelve o'clock at night, and has no right to sell on Sunday.

The CHAIRMAN. — Did they keep a proper book or register?

A. No, sir.

Q. Is not an innholder required to do that?

A. Yes, sir. That is one of the reasons why we refused his license.

By Mr. HART. — After you had refused him an innholder's license, you went on to give him a license as a victualler. When you came to that, did you give Mr. Crosby a fair show to come in?

A. You are speaking to me now as one of the members of the Board?

Q. Yes, sir.

A. I don't know.

Q. Did he ever have any notice?

A. I don't know, sir.

Q. It seems to me, as far as we can learn, it was a matter that was sprung upon him.

A. Well, you see if the estate which he represented was not an adjoining estate, under the law he had no right to make any technical objection, and the Board had decided, on consultation with the City Solicitor, that that was not an adjoining estate; therefore legal objection could not be made by Mr. Crosby, and the single question was whether he should have a license.

Col. WALKER. — I do not know whether he had any chance or not; but if the whole of the case for the opposition was developed on the first hearing we might not feel it advisable to go over the whole thing again. The chairman asked a question about innholders. You know you cannot carry out the old English idea of the common law, for the simple reason that the whole manners, habits, and customs of the people have changed since the common law doctrine was in vogue. Then every man owned his house; but now I think one-third of the population of Boston reside in rooms, and get their meals outside of their houses. These people must be fed, and an innholder's license is granted in some places to assist that class of people. The man who takes a glass of ale on Monday, Tuesday, Wednesday, Thursday, Friday, and Saturday, wants it equally as well on Sunday, and certainly there is no reason in honesty why he should not have it. And that is the reason why this class of innholders and common victuallers have so rapidly increased, because so many people living in this way get their food outside. You would be surprised at the number of little restaurants with two, three, four, or five tables that are open, doing a *bona fide* business, furnishing food to people who live in rooms and flats.

Mr. HERSEY. — If I draw the proper inference, all it is necessary for a person to do, if the owner of the adjoining estate objects to his having a victualler's license, is to convey, lease, or sell a strip of his own estate, and that places him outside of the statute, and the commissioners then would not consider at all the objection of the estate which had before adjoined?

Col. WALKER. — If a man makes a *bona fide* sale of a part of his property, it takes it out of the law in relation to adjoining estates; and as a matter of technical law, the commissioners might not consider the objection. They might go on and consider other testimony.

Mr. HERSEY. — Is it not an evasion of the law?

Col. WALKER. — We must take the law as we find it.

Mr. HERSEY. — Should you consider that they placed themselves outside of the law if it turns upon an evasion?

Col. WALKER. — Suppose a case where there is no objection except my own. I object to the granting of a license, because I am an adjoining owner. Then the man objected to sell ten inches or twenty feet of his estate. Then the adjoining owner, who protested, is not the adjoining owner in law. Now, suppose we say we wont't grant that license, because the adjoining owner protests; then we come face to face between a falsehood and the law, right off.

Mr. HERSEY. — Then, it is not true, as you first stated, that an adjoining estate always has power to prevent the issuing of a license?

Col. WALKER. — Not when it ceases to be an adjoining estate. The adjoining estate has that power; but when it ceases to be an adjoining estate, it cannot have the power.

Mr. HERSEY. — So that the party who wishes to obtain a license, and is objected to by an adjoining estate, can make that estate not an adjoining one, by evasion?

Col. WALKER. — Precisely.

Mr. HERSEY. — Then it is not true that because I own an estate adjoining one where liquor is sold that I can stop the man's license, because he can sell a strip of land —

Col. WALKER. — And you no longer join.

Mr. HERSEY. — So the law is really inoperative?

A. There are a good many things in the law that are simply foolish.

Mr. HERSEY. — It seems to me that the duty of the commissioners would be to decide that, in a case where they place themselves outside of the statute for this evasion, they should not have a license.

Col. WALKER. — Then you would have the commissioners act as the law makers or law givers of the Commonwealth?

Mr. HERSEY. — No ; it is within your power, and you can do as you will about it.

Major JONES. — Let me just state what our practice has been in these cases. I have three in mind now, and I will give one particularly. Adjoining the Dudley-street Baptist Church is a building that is directly opposite the head-quarters of the Highland passengers. There is a long wall in front of the church. The second wall is owned by a man named Fallon, who has kept a liquor shop there a good many years. When this law went into effect some of the people who were personal acquaintances of mine called my attention to it, and wanted to know if there was not some way to stop it. I referred them to the statute. They filed their objection, and, after various expedients had been resorted to — the commission still rejecting the application — as a legal dodge, the attorney for the applicant suggested that a strip of that land should be sold ; and they came and presented to us a deed, duly executed and recorded, of ten feet of their property to another party. But we, regarding the thing as simply an evasion of the law, said that whether this was an evasion or not — I said it, and the commission agreed with me that I might say it — it would not make any difference whether you sold or not, you could not have a license for a liquor shop alongside of a church, connecting with church property, so long as I sit on the Board, if I can prevent it.

The CHAIRMAN. — You did not apply the same thing in this case?

Major JONES. — There was another case in South Boston, and another at Jamaica Plain, where they undertook to do the same thing, and we rejected the applications.

Col. WALKER. — We never rejected them because it was an adjoining estate after the estate had been divided.

The CHAIRMAN. — You did not look at the paper to see whether it had been conveyed in this case?

Major JONES. — No, sir, we did not.

The CHAIRMAN. — You knew this place was here, where they have services all through the week?

Major JONES. — Well, the Sunday business was objected to because of the sale of liquor. Mr. Crosby said they might sell food by the ton, he did not object to that ; and when we gave them a license which allowed them to sell food, that objection was overcome. Now, I do not want Mr. Gove to confuse this with the Young Women's Christian Association case. I think the chairman will agree with me that there never has been an application for appointment on the police force, or an application for a license, or any other thing that ever came before the Board, which was so strenuously urged as the granting of a license to Murray ; and the license was refused upon this ground. The government of the Young Women's Christian Association complained, not of Mr. Murray, but that it was a place around which men resorted. Most all the young ladies at that institution are school teachers, clerks, shop girls, and the like, and most of them were obliged to pass his corner ; and they had repeatedly been annoyed by men under the influence of intoxicating liquor. They made that objection. They came to us, appeared splendidly, presented their evidence in a very nice and substantial way, and we rejected that license ; and from that time down to this, men, societies, and, I was going to say, every member of the City Government — you would be astonished ; they would fill nearly every room in this building — have come and threatened and bulldozed, and tried in every possible way to induce us to give that man a license. And now they have undertaken to seek communion right across on the other side ; and they are here to-day with all sorts of threats and intimidations about that license. We say no. The license was rejected for good cause, and we will not insult those women, who are obliged to pass that way, to and from their meals. We wonder why they have not been here before.

Mr. GOVE. — Somebody spoke to me in reference to it.

Major JONES. — If ever I voted strenuously it was for that.

Mr. HERSEY. — The conditions in this case are not very different.

Major JONES. — Oh, yes. You see there is a blank wall to the corporation's establishment. Then they have an enclosed yard on the other side of the house, and the children are not allowed to go outside.

Mr. HERSEY. — They have to pass by to get there.

Major JONES. — No ; they live there.

Mr. HERSEY. — I am speaking of the children at school.

Major JONES. — Well, there are liquor shops in all parts of the city.

Mr. HERSEY. — They congregate right around this one, don't they ?

Major JONES. — No, sir. [Explains the location in question.] Mr. Crosby is a very fine man, and he is engaged in a splendid mission. I am glad he made his objection ; and if he wants to have the license broken, I hope the Court will do it.

The CHAIRMAN. — I hope they will try it. They are indorsed by Henry P. Kidder and Samuel B. Cruft.

Major JONES. — By the way, there is one piece of evidence you ought to have. Mr. Crosby, you will remember, signs that protest as in behalf of the board of directors. Of course, Mr. Crosby himself has no authority ; but, at a meeting of the Board, they voted to instruct him to do this. Mr. Whitmore said he had seen a member of that Board, who stated that he had been present, as far as he knew, at every meeting, and no such vote had ever been passed. Of course, we told Mr. Crosby that ; but we took it to be just as he said : that it was done by a solemn vote of the committee.

Mr. GOVE. — And he went and saw the same man that Mr. Whitmore saw, and he said that he told Mr. Whitmore that the date of the objection was the day of the meeting of the Board ; that he was not present ; but, if he had been present, he should have voted for it, and he had no doubt such a thing had been done.

Col. WALKER. — We will give you the names of these gentlemen, and the evidence, so far as it was secured by the clerk in making his abstract. And if either of you should come to us and make a statement, we should consider it was worthy of consideration.

POLICE IN AMERICA

An Arno Press/New York Times Collection

Missouri Joint Committee of the General Assembly.
Report of the Joint Committee of the General Assembly Appointed to Investigate the Police Department of the City of St. Louis. St. Louis, Missouri, 1868.

National Commission on Law Observance and Enforcement.
Report on the Police. Washington, D. C., 1931.

National Prison Association.
Proceedings of the Annual Congress of the National Prison Association of the United States: Selected Articles. 1874–1902.

New York City Common Council.
Report of the Special Committee of the New York City Board of Aldermen on the New York City Police Department. New York, 1844.

National Police Convention.
Official Proceedings of the National Prison Convention. St. Louis, 1871.

Pennsylvania Federation of Labor.
The American Cossack. Washington, D. C., 1915.

Police and the Blacks: U.S. Civil Rights Commission Hearings. 1960–1966.

Police in New York City: An Investigation. New York, 1912–1931.

The President's Commission on Law Enforcement and Administration of Justice.
Task Force Report: The Police. Washington, D. C., 1967.

Sellin, Thorsten, editor.
The Police and the Crime Problem. Philadelphia, 1929.

Smith, Bruce, editor.
New Goals in Police Management. Philadelphia, 1954.

Sprogle, Howard O.
The Philadelphia Police, Past and Present. Philadelphia, 1887.

U.S. Committee on Education and Labor.
The Chicago Memorial Day Incident: Hearings and Report. Washington, D. C., 1937.

U.S. Committee on Education and Labor.
Documents Relating to Intelligence Bureau or Red Squad of Los Angeles Police Department. Washington, D. C., 1940.

U.S. Committee on Education and Labor.
Private Police Systems. Washington, D. C., 1939.

Urban Police: Selected Surveys. 1926–1946.

Women's Suffrage and the Police: Three Senate Documents. Washington, D. C., 1913.

Woods, Arthur.
Crime Prevention. Princeton, New Jersey, 1918.

Woods, Arthur.
Policeman and Public. New Haven, Conn., 1919.

AMERICAN POLICE SUPPLEMENT

International Association of Chiefs of Police.
Proceedings of the Annual Conventions of the International Association of Chiefs of Police. 1893–1930. 5 vols.

New York State Senate.
Report and Proceedings of the Senate Committee Appointed to Investigate the Police Department of the City of New York. (Lexow Committee Report). New York, 1895. 6 vols.

THE POLICE IN GREAT BRITAIN

Committee on Police Conditions of Service.
Report of the Committee on Police Conditions of Service. London, 1949.

Committee on the Police Service.
Minutes of Evidence and Report: England, Wales, Scotland. London, 1919–1920.

Royal Commission on Police Powers and Procedures.
Report of the Royal Commission on Police Powers and Procedure. London, 1929.

Select Committee on Police.
Report of Select Committee on Police with the Minutes of Evidence. London, 1853.

Royal Commission Upon the Duties of the Metropolitan Police.
Minutes of Evidence Taken Before the Royal Commission Upon the Duties of the Metropolitan Police Together With Appendices and Index. London, 1908.

Committee on Police.
Report from the Select Committee on Police of the Metropolis. London, 1828.